Introduction to the Organ

INTRODUCTION TO THE
ORGAN

by
AUSTIN NILAND

Foreword by
FRANCIS JACKSON

FABER AND FABER
24 Russell Square
London

First published in 1968
by Faber and Faber Limited
24 Russell Square London WC1
Printed in Great Britain by
Ebenezer Baylis and Son, Ltd
The Trinity Press, Worcester, and London
All rights reserved

S.B.N. 571 08737 X

for

ELIZABETH

'But oh! what art can teach,
What human voice can reach
The sacred organ's praise?'

DRYDEN: *A Song for St Cecilia's Day*

Foreword

by Dr Francis Jackson

Organist of York Minster

It is now fifteen years since the organ in the Royal Festival Hall, London—that much discussed and most controversial of instruments—was installed. This notable event, which heralded the dawn of a new era in British organ building, has probably influenced the subsequent style of British organs more than any other in the long and diverse history of the art. It has also stimulated interest in the organ and its repertoire to an extent unknown since the Victorian era.

The kind of organ that held sway from the closing years of Victoria's reign until the end of the Second World War had given good service in church and town hall, but by 1946 it was due for review. Because of the increase of specialization in all branches of music and the growing ease with which music of earlier periods could be heard in its true medium, dissatisfaction was increasingly felt over the inadequacy of the average British organ to give an adequate account of it.

The classical organ was then all but completely unknown in Britain, and the controversy which raged between its adherents and those of the romantic organ, did so mainly as a result of the ignorance of the majority of British organists. But after it had died down, the neo-classical organ gradually began to replace the romantic one; and minds were awakened to the possibilities latent not only in the baroque organs of Germany, but also in

ix

those of France, Spain, Holland and Denmark, and the miraculously preserved historical masterpieces of Zion, Hillerod, Cappel, Weingarten, Haarlem and many others. People have in fact been unable to gainsay the evidence of their ears, and have been obliged to award the palm to the classical organ. The sheer beauty of the voicing, and the vitality and impact of the best examples have gained it the allegiance of an increasing body of players and listeners. Moreover, its economy—the fact that a classical organ can be less than half the size of a romantic one and yet be equally or more effective—has appealed to those who have to pay the bills.

The opponents of the classical revival feared, more than anything, that a unique 'Englishness' would disappear from their organs: and certainly there was much that it was desirable not to lose. One aspect of this 'Englishness'—the romantic approach to tonal design—has certainly been replaced by something of greater value for the needs of the present day. But this has not made it impossible or difficult to play the romantic repertoire. On the contrary, the latter has benefited through the vitality of classical voicing and choruses. Yet there is no lack of traditional national character in our classical revival organs. The Hill, the Walker and the Willis of the pre-electric action period were lineal descendants of Dallam, Smith, Harris, Snetzler and Green, and the best neo-classical essays have been carried on in that tradition. The British full swell is still a very potent feature: rightly so because of its extreme usefulness and its unique, exciting quality. Mutations, very much in evidence during the seventeenth and eighteenth centuries, are now reinstated. Low wind pressures are again employed, to the great benefit of the choruses and of the voicing generally. Nor are string tone and the quieter romantic voices neglected. 'The modern British organ', as the author says in this book, 'is looked upon as an eclectic instrument embracing the essentials of all important organ-building periods, yet retaining a unique national character'.

In this book the organ of Britain, the author's own country, is naturally taken as the norm, but the organs of other countries

Foreword

are none the less most faithfully dealt with, and in perspective. The book is filled with things that every organist should know; things which will increase his vision and widen his horizons. But most important of all, these things will contribute towards the musical purpose of the instrument which is, after all, the reason for its existence. The knowledge the reader will gain cannot fail to be helpful in improving his approach to whatever school of music he is interested in playing.

An organist must be an improviser, not only of sound, but also of colour. An organ, more than any other musical instrument, is an individual, and the labels on the stop knobs can never be taken for granted. The player must be quite sure, before starting, what kind of sound he wants. He must then be prepared to continue searching for it, even among the most unlikely stops, until he finds the exact tone colour or the nearest approximation. Just as every organ has a different palette, so have the various schools of composition. The field is vast, and much study must be done to acquire a full knowledge of it. Those who start with this book will build on a sure foundation.

Contents

Contents

Contents

Part II Use of the Organ

Contents

Part III Select Glossary of Organ Stops

List of Illustrations

Plates

List of Illustrations
Figures

Preface

The purpose of this book is to provide for the organ student, particularly the beginner, such essential information about the construction, history and practical use of the organ as will help him to play it artistically and intelligently.

Several teachers of the organ have led the author to believe that a book of this kind is greatly needed. Obviously, much of the information it contains can be procured by delving into the large bibliography on the organ, a selection from which is given at the end of this book. But where should the student be advised to begin? How best to explain the many technicalities of this most complex and diverse of all musical instruments? These problems confront the conscientious teacher. The author hopes that many teachers, necessarily preoccupied with their main task of guiding their pupils through the problems of interpretation and technique, will welcome a book which presumes to undertake the labour of technical and historical indoctrination on their behalf.

He also hopes that, at a time when the organ is becoming rehabilitated as a serious musical instrument, the book will be of value to the general reader who wishes to learn something about it.

It has been thought wisest to start with the assumption that the reader has no previous knowledge of the organ at all—though it is assumed that he has the elementary musical knowledge that a good teacher would expect him to have acquired before embarking upon a study of the organ. From this basic point the author has sought to lead the reader through the

Preface

complexities of the organ in its various forms, step by step, logically and directly, using the simplest possible language and explaining each technical term as it arises, but introducing no unnecessary technicalities.

With these objects in mind the book has been planned in two main parts (Parts I and II), the first describing the instrument itself, and the second dealing with its use in music. Thus, Part I begins by explaining the essential nature of the organ and its workings. Then follows naturally an account of how tone is generated in organ pipes, and how it is compounded into choruses and ultimately incorporated into the tonal structure of the British organ; and at this stage the console arrangement and method of control of various British organs are conveniently outlined.

Part II is concerned with practical considerations of registration and musical use. The organ repertoire extends from the fourteenth century to modern times, and the modern approach to interpretation is an historical one. Thus if the student is to play any of this music intelligently, he will need knowledge—of the tonal characteristics of the organs for which musicians of the past have composed, and of how best to realize their music on whatever kind of organ may be at his disposal. For this reason, Part II begins by outlining the nature of the important past schools of organ building and contemporary registrational practice as an essential background to proffering guidance on the use of the average British organ—the kind of instrument the student is most likely to encounter—and the performance on it of various kinds of music.

The book ends with a concise glossary of organ stops (Part III), both to fill in the gaps and to help the reader in his general understanding of the historical background.

Descriptions of organ mechanisms have been kept to a minimum and introduced only where strictly relevant to musical use. Thus, the workings of the four main key-actions to be found in organs today are described in some detail because they are germane to the understanding of differences of touch and musical response. On the other hand, fascinating by-ways such

Preface

as Kegellade and Pitman windchests, and details of electro-
pneumatic drawstop actions, have not been touched upon, and
are left for the curious reader to explore elsewhere, should he
so desire.

The problem of describing the tonal structure of the British
organ (Part I) has not been an easy one to solve; and since the
method adopted may not be to the liking of everyone, a few
words of explanation are necessary. The difficulty arises because
of the present transitional state of British organ building.

Had this book been written at almost any other point in
organ history the task of describing the contemporary organ
and its use would have been relatively easy. In seventeenth-
or eighteenth-century Germany and France, for example,
or eighteenth-century England, or nineteenth-century France,
organs were designed on what were regarded as irrevocably
established principles. Registrational practice was neatly codi-
fied. But in the late 1960s, taste in British organ building is
changing from 'romantic' to 'classical'. The classical revival
has gained a firm hold, but its zenith is by no means in sight.
New organs are being built and old ones tonally remodelled
with tonal schemes incorporating various degrees of classicism.
Yet many 'romantic' organs survive, and no doubt will continue to do so, together with some Victorian and older organs
which may broadly be termed 'classical'.

How in the midst of all this confusion can the tonal structure
of the British organ best be outlined? The author has decided
that the most satisfactory approach is to take as a norm the
general-purpose type of organ with a strong classical basis
(such as he believes is now fairly generally accepted) and then
to describe its characteristics, showing how they differ from
some of the less happy features which continue to survive in
romantic tonal schemes. Complete objectivity in an under-
taking of this kind is, of course, impossible. But at all times
the intention has been to describe the British organ as it *is,*
and not to make a case for the organ of the future—and the ways
in which the author, or anyone else, might personally wish to
see it develop.

Preface

No apology whatsoever is made for the fact that this book is written by an amateur—in the sense of one who studies and plays the organ for the love of it, not to earn a living. Most books about the organ, in English at any rate, have been written by such amateurs. Few professional organists or organ builders, seem to have the time or the inclination for authorship though their specialist knowledge in their respective spheres may exceed that of the amateur. The bibliography of the organ might well be richer if this were not so.

The author wishes to record his indebtedness to the following, and to express his sincere thanks for the help they have given: to Nicholas Danby Esq for the original idea; to Messrs Harrison & Harrison Ltd, William Hill & Son and Norman & Beard Ltd, N. P. Mander Ltd and J. W. Walker & Sons Ltd for the provision of photographs and permission to use them; to N. P. Mander Ltd for so generously providing the line drawings; to Dr W. L. Sumner for permission to reproduce the two A. G. Hill drawings; to Miss Eileen Bridge, Michael Gillingham Esq and Brian S. Quilter Esq for reading the book in typescript and making many valuable suggestions for its improvement; and finally to his daughter Elizabeth for help in preparing the index.

AUSTIN NILAND
August 1967

PART I

MECHANICAL AND TONAL
STRUCTURE

I

Construction and Workings

The Essential Organ

Like all complex things the organ is easiest understood by thinking of it in its simplest form. What essentially is an organ? To answer this is to answer the question: what were the earliest organs like? The essential organ consists of a single scale of pipes planted on a chest filled with wind under pressure, the admission of which to the pipes is under the mechanical control of a performer. The earliest organs were of this kind—the smallest possible organ unit. Larger organs are simply multiples of such units.

Once the basic organ was invented, some two thousand years ago, it was a series of logical steps first to provide two, three, or more pipes to each note; then to provide 'stops' for shutting off sets of pipes not required at any particular time; and then, for reasons of convenience or tonal contrast, to arrange two or more organs with their keyboards in tiers so that they could be controlled by the hands and feet of one performer. This process of evolution is described in Part II. All that need be understood for the time being is that despite differences of size and scope, all organs are basically the same, and that a large organ is only several smaller organs in one.

A Small Organ Explained

Figure 1—a cross-section of a straightforward small organ of

3

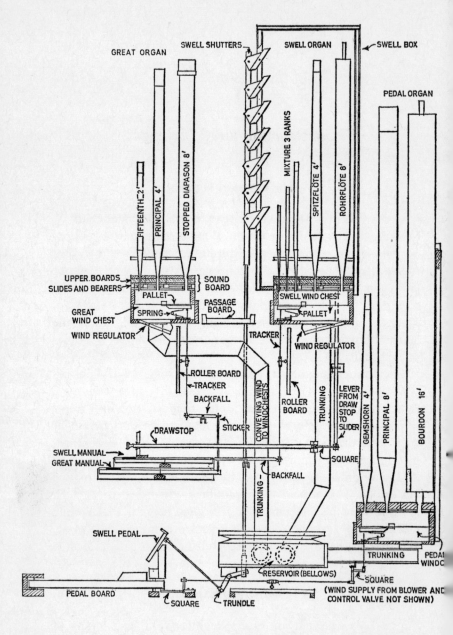

GREAT ORGAN

SWELL SHUTTERS

SWELL ORGAN

SWELL BOX

PEDAL ORGAN

FIFTEENTH 2'

PRINCIPAL 4'

STOPPED DIAPASON 8'

MIXTURE 3 RANKS

SPITZFLÖTE 4'

ROHRFLÖTE 8'

GEMSHORN 4'

PRINCIPAL 8'

BOURDON 16'

UPPER BOARDS
SLIDES AND BEARERS
SOUND BOARD
PALLET
GREAT WIND CHEST
PASSAGE BOARD
SPRING
WIND REGULATOR
SWELL WIND CHEST
PALLET
WIND REGULATOR

TRACKER

ROLLER BOARD
TRACKER
BACKFALL

CONVEYING WIND TO WINDCHESTS

ROLLER BOARD

TRUNKING

LEVER FROM DRAW STOP TO SLIDER

DRAWSTOP

STICKER

SQUARE

SWELL MANUAL
GREAT MANUAL

TRUNKING

BACKFALL

SWELL PEDAL

RESERVOIR (BELLOWS)

SQUARE

TRUNKING

PEDAL WINDC

PEDAL BOARD

SQUARE

TRUNDLE

(WIND SUPPLY FROM BLOWER AND CONTROL VALVE NOT SHOWN)

4

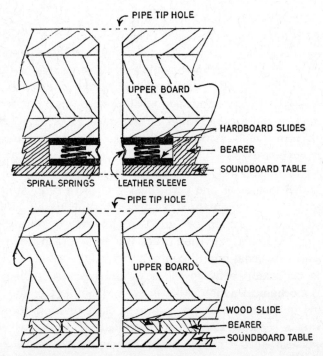

PIPE TIP HOLE

UPPER BOARD

HARDBOARD SLIDES

BEARER

SOUNDBOARD TABLE

SPIRAL SPRINGS   LEATHER SLEEVE

PIPE TIP HOLE

UPPER BOARD

WOOD SLIDE

BEARER

SOUNDBOARD TABLE

1A. Two soundboard cross-sections showing the position of a slider below a pipe-tip hole. The lower diagram shows a traditional wooden slider. The upper one illustrates a modern inner-sprung slider which ensures a really tight fit and no leakage of wind.

1. (*opposite*) Diagrammatic cross-section of a small two-manual and pedal organ with tracker action, illustrating the basic construction and working of the organ. A few details, including the manual and pedal coupling action, are omitted for clarity. The 'roller-board' is a device for conveying the key-action movement laterally — necessary because it is not possible for the pipes to stand directly above their respective keys: see also Plate III. The 'wind regulators' (small bellows-like attachments to the windchests) contract when there is a sudden demand upon the wind supply and compensate for the loss. For details of the slider action, see the soundboard cross-section in Figure 1A.

two manuals and pedals—illustrates the principle on which all organs are constructed. Some details have been omitted for clarity. The names of the stops and the various pipe shapes can be disregarded for the time being; these also are explained later. The cross-section, of course, only shows the position at one note. The keys, pipes and 'action' (the mechanism connecting the keys to the pipes) should be imagined as being repeated three-dimensionally as often as there are notes to the compass of the keyboards.

This imaginary organ contains three organs or 'divisions' under the control of one performer, each with three stops or 'registers'. The lower manual (keyboard for the hands) controls the pipes of the main or 'great' organ; the upper manual controls a secondary division called the 'swell' organ; the pedal keyboard or 'pedal-board' controls the pedal organ.

The connexion between the keys and pipes is 'tracker' or direct mechanical action—the oldest and simplest of the four actions in current use. The pipes of each division stand in holes on a separate soundboard (see Plate X) below which is a windchest filled with air under pressure conveyed through wind trunking from the reservoir and blowing plant. Below the pipes of each note is a hinged valve or 'pallet' held shut by the 'pallet spring'. Each key is connected to its pallet by a series of 'stickers', 'trackers' and 'squares'. Depression of the key pulls down the pallet and lets the wind into the pipes, causing them to speak. It is from this 'opening' function that the 'key' derives its name.

The player can select the sets of pipes needed at any particular time by pulling out 'drawstops'. Each drawstop is connected by a system of rods to a 'slider'—a perforated strip of wood running in a groove below the feet of each set of pipes. When the drawstop is pulled out the holes in the slider correspond with the footholes of the pipes so that the wind can get in when the keys are depressed. Pushing in the drawstop moves the slider so that the perforations no longer correspond with the footholes and the wind is excluded, even though the pallets may be open.

A Small Organ Explained

It is easy to see how the term 'stop' originated—a name given to a device for stopping off the wind from a particular rank of pipes. Its modern usage is often imprecise. Generally the term is taken to mean a particular set of pipes controlled by one drawstop (e.g., the principal, Spitzflöte or mixture shown in Figure 1). Strictly, these are 'speaking stops', since they directly produce sound. But the term is also applied to other mechanical devices which, although operated by drawstops, do not directly control sets of pipes. The most important of these are 'couplers'.

The main function of couplers, as the term implies, is to join together two or more divisions of an organ. Our imaginary organ is provided with three standard couplers worked by drawstops labelled 'swell to great', 'great to pedal' and 'swell to pedal'. The working of these cannot be clearly shown in a two-dimensional diagram, though it is quite simple. When no couplers are in use the stops of a particular division can only be played from their own keyboard; for instance, the swell Spitzflöte, Rohrflöte and mixture can only be played on the upper manual. Pulling out the 'swell to great' coupler, however, enables all the swell stops to be played from the great organ keys. Thus, the entire manual resources of the instrument can be controlled from the great keyboard. The 'great to pedal' and 'swell to pedal' couplers likewise make the corresponding notes of the great and swell manuals playable from the pedalboard. In tracker action organs, such as we are now considering, the couplers actually pull down the keys of the coupled manual. With later actions (to be discussed shortly) the coupled keys are not moved.

Organ pipes speak only at the constant volume given to them by the voicer and are incapable of the kind of expression peculiar to orchestral instruments. But a kind of *crescendo, diminuendo* and *sforzando* can be obtained by means of the 'swell box'. Figure 1 shows the pipes of the swell organ enclosed in a wooden box, the front of which is fitted with louvres or shutters like a Venetian blind. (When this device was first fitted to harpsichords during the second half of the eighteenth century it was known as the 'Venetian swell'.) Opening and closing the swell shutters by means of the 'swell pedal' regulates the amount of sound emission and simulates the crescendo and diminuendo effects. It is from this swelling of sound that the swell organ—the first division of the British organ to be so treated—derived its name. A division treated in this way is said to be 'enclosed'. Divisions such as the great and pedal organs of Figure 1 which stand on open soundboards are said to be 'unenclosed'. Other divisions, such as the choir and solo organs (to be explained later), are frequently enclosed in swell boxes in addition to the swell organ.

It will now be clear that a larger organ than the one just described could be obtained simply by adding basic units and perhaps extra mechanical complications. For instance, Figure 1 can be imagined as being extended to include three, four, or even five manual divisions instead of two, with many more stops to each, and a larger pedal division. The simple mechanical connexion between drawstops and sliders, keys and pallets, swell pedal and shutters could be replaced by more complex electrical and pneumatic machinery. The drawstops could give way to small ivory tabs functioning as electrical switches. Even the simple slider windchests could be superseded. Yet the general principle of the organ would remain the same.

The Importance of Key Action

Although the organ is a musical instrument it is also, unavoidably, a machine. To play it intelligently requires some knowledge of its workings, in the same way that a good driver needs to be aware of what is happening inside his motor car when he changes gear or applies the brakes.

Many people are bored by mechanical matters, and it is not the author's intention to dwell on the mechanical aspects of the organ any more than is absolutely necessary. One aspect however must claim our attention in some detail—the mechanical connexion between pallets and keys.

When asked to play a strange organ one of the first questions an experienced organist will ask is 'What kind of action does it have?' Because the key action is the sole medium whereby the sounds of organ pipes are turned into music, it is of the greatest imaginable importance and must be discussed in some detail.

Four types of key action are in current use—tracker (just described), pneumatic-lever, tubular-pneumatic and electro-pneumatic—all of which vary considerably in touch and musical response. In the same way that a good pianist needs to be aware of the intricacies of pianoforte action and its bearing on touch and tone production, so the organist should know what kind of action he is using, broadly how it works, and its artistic merits in relation to the other systems. This is the purpose of what follows.

Tracker Action

It has been seen from Figure 1 that tracker action consists of a direct mechanical connexion of rods, levers and wires. It is as old as the organ itself and was in universal use until about 1840; but like the Gothic style in architecture it never completely died out and has undergone a process of revival.

Tracker is the most responsive and sensitive of all actions—at least, under the right working conditions. It works best in small, compact organs, or where the divisions are arranged vertically and the force of gravity can aid the balance and downward movement of the parts. Because of the direct connexion the attack and release of the sound are simultaneous with touch, and the speed of pallet opening is related to the speed of key depression. The organist can thus exercise an element of control over the admission of wind to the pipes and—provided they are sensitively voiced and he has sufficient skill—vary their attack by touch. In this way tracker action conveys individuality of touch as no other action can.

Good tracker action has an easily recognizable feel. The pallet spring tension and the wind pressure require the finger to exert slightly more weight in putting the key down the first eighth of an inch or so than to hold it down in its bed. This creates a feeling of 'top resistance' (rather like the plucking touch of a harpsichord) which is not only very pleasing but makes for a feeling of intimacy between the player and the source of sound. Good tracker touch is light and not too 'deep'. Even with couplers drawn it need not be uncomfortably heavy, as large vertically disposed organs in Holland and Germany have proved.

After about 1840 new voicing and constructional methods involving higher pressures of wind, non-vertical layouts and greater use of couplers combined to make tracker action uncomfortably heavy in largish organs. This led to the development of new, lighter actions, though tracker continued in use for small and medium-sized organs throughout the nineteenth century and later.

Pneumatic-lever Action

The first new action was pneumatic-lever or 'Barker lever' action, as it is usually called after Charles Spackman Barker (1804–1879) who was concerned with its development. It was first used by the French organ builder Cavaillé-Coll in 1842 and became the main action for large French organs throughout the rest of the century. The only difference between pneumatic-lever and tracker is that a pneumatic motor, a sort of small leather bellows, which moves when inflated with air, is interposed near the final stage of the system to do the heavy work of pulling open the pallet (Figure 1). Pneumatic-lever touch consequently retains much of the positive feel of tracker, and many people consider it to be the next best thing, though there is no control over the speed of pallet opening and the intimacy of good tracker action is missing. Its main defect is a tendency to be noisy in operation.

Tubular-pneumatic Action

In tubular-pneumatic action the pneumatic-lever system is carried a stage further: the direct connexion is completely replaced by tubes of pressurized air. It was first developed in France during the mid-nineteenth century, then adopted and brought to a high standard of efficiency by the nineteenth-

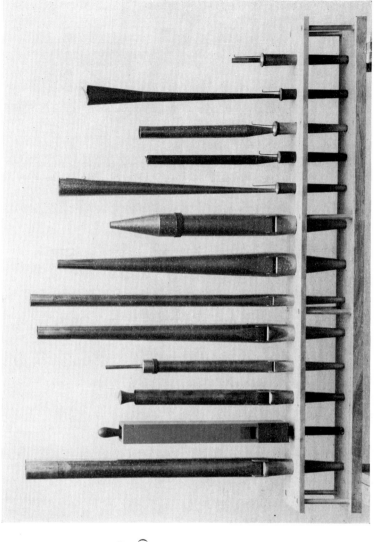

I. Specimen flue and reed pipes.
From left to right:
(1) open diapason
(2) stopped diapason (wood)
(3) stopped diapason (metal)
(4) Spitzflöte
(5) Rohrflöte
(6) dulciana
(7) Gemshorn
(8) Koppelflöte
(9) trumpet (full length resonator)
(10) and (11) clarinet and
Krumhorn (half-length resonators)
(12) oboe (full length resonator)
(13) regal (fractional length
resonator).
All these pipes sound the same
note, 2 ft C.

PIPES STANDING ABOVE

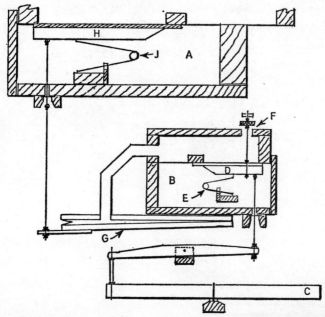

2. Pneumatic-lever action. The action is shown in the 'off' position. The windchest (A) and valve box (B) are filled with air under pressure. When the key (C) is depressed the action works in the same manner as tracker action up to the point of opening the primary pallet-valve (D) against the tension of its spring (E). This closes the exhaust valve (F) and opens the way for the wind to inflate the power-pneumatic motor (G). The downward movement of this pulls open the main pallet (H) against the tension of its spring (J), and admits the wind to the pipes. Release of the key (C) cuts off the supply of pressure air from the motor (G), and the pallet (H) is able to close under the tension of its spring.

century British organ builder Henry Willis.* There are two forms: the pressure or charge system (Figure 3) and the exhaust system (Figure 4). Well made pneumatic action of either kind is very responsive but without the positive feel of tracker. The

* 'Father' Henry Willis (1821–1901), one of the greatest of the nineteenth-century British organ builders, whose work is discussed in Chapter VI, page 125. Like his great Restoration period predecessor, 'Father' Bernard Smith (see page 115), he was canonised 'Father' by popular consent, partly to distinguish him from his younger relatives, but mainly in recognition of his great artistic worth.

touch is often unnaturally light with no top resistance; but the couplers work without moving the keys of the coupled manuals, and no more weight is needed to play on full organ than on a

PIPES STANDING ABOVE

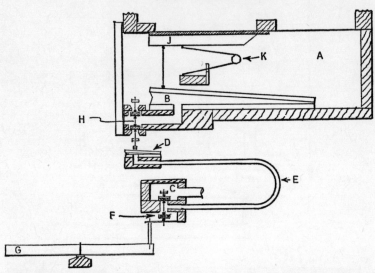

3. Tubular-pneumatic action, pressure or charge system. The action is shown in the 'off' position. The windchest (A), the power-pneumatic motor (B) and the key valve-chest (C) are filled with air under pressure. The key valve-chest (C) is connected to the primary pneumatic motor (D) by the pneumatic tubing (E). The primary motor (D) is in a position of collapse because the lower end of the tubing is open to the outer atmosphere through the valve (F). Depression of the key (G) moves the valve (F) upwards so that the pneumatic tubing is at once sealed to the outer atmosphere and open to the air pressure in the key valve-chest (C), which then travels up the tubing and inflates the primary motor (D). This in turn moves the valve (H) so that the supply of pressure air is cut off from the power motor (B), and simultaneously the air within it is exhausted into the outer atmosphere. The power motor (B) then collapses under the air pressure in the windchest (A) pulling open the main pallet (J) against the tension of its spring (K) and admitting the wind to the pipes. Release of the key returns the valve (F) to the 'off' position, opening the tubing to the outer atmosphere, and the train of events is reversed.

single stop. The console* can be detached from the pipes to an extent not possible with the earlier actions. Second-rate or worn pneumatic actions, however, are sluggish both in attack

* The keyboards and stop controls (see p. 68).

The Importance of Key Action

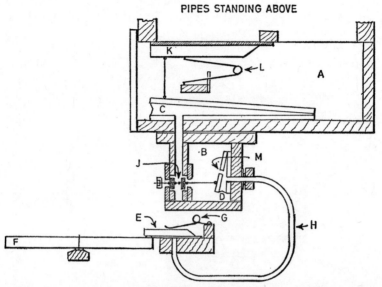

4. Tubular-pneumatic action, exhaust system. The action is shown in the 'off' position. The windchest (A) is filled with air under pressure. The primary action box (B) is also filled with pressurized air which charges the power pneumatic motor (C) and the primary pneumatic motor (D) through the small 'bleed hole' (M). The action box is sealed from the outer atmosphere by the position of the pallet-valve (E). Depression of the key (F) raises the pallet-valve (E) against the tension of its spring (G), enabling the pressure air in the primary motor (D) to exhaust into the outer atmosphere through the pneumatic tubing (H). Then the primary motor (D), collapsing under the pressure of the air in the action box (B), moves the valve (J) which simultaneously cuts off the supply of pressure air from the power motor (C) and enables the air inside it to exhaust into the outer atmosphere. Then the power motor (C), collapsing under the air pressure in the windchest (A), pulls open the main pallet (K) against the pressure of its spring (L) and admits the wind to the pipes. Release of the key (F), allows the pallet-valve (E) to close, sealing the primary motor (D) from the outer atmosphere. The primary motor (D) is then recharged through the 'bleed hole' (M) and the train of events is reversed.

and release and present an insuperable obstacle to clear playing. They have probably done more to damage the reputation of the organ than any other single factor.

Electro-pneumatic Action

With electro-pneumatic action the connexion between the key and pallet-opening mechanism is a pair of electric wires.

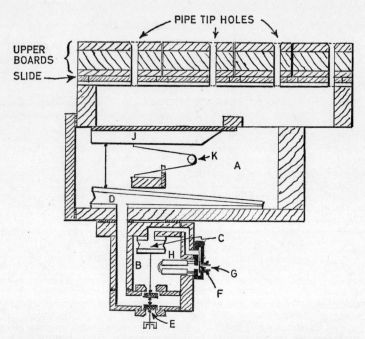

5. Electro-pneumatic action, slider chest. The action is shown in the 'off' position. The windchest (A) is charged with air under pressure. The primary action box (B) is also filled with pressurized air which charges the primary pneumatic motor (C) and the power pneumatic motor (D). The pressure air in (B), (C) and (D) is sealed from the outer atmosphere by the position of the valve (E) and the magnet disc-valve armature (F) which is held by a low-tension spring against the escape windway (G). Depression of the key (not shown) closes a low voltage electric circuit which energizes the electro-magnet (H). The disc-valve armature (F) is then drawn towards the poles of the magnet, simultaneously sealing off the supply of pressure air from the primary motor (C) and opening the escape windway (G), thus allowing the air in the primary motor (C) to exhaust into the outer atmosphere. The primary motor (C) then collapses under the air pressure in the action box (B). This moves the valve (E) so that it simultaneously cuts off the supply of pressure air from the power motor (D) and allows the air within it to exhaust into the outer atmosphere. The power motor (D) then collapses under the air pressure in the windchest (A) and pulls open the main pallet (J) against the tension of its spring (K), admitting the wind to the pipes. Release of the key opens the electric circuit, de-energizes the magnet and reverses the series of events.

The Importance of Key Action

The key is a switch that closes an electric circuit. This energizes an electro-magnet which triggers off the pneumatic pallet-opening mechanism.

The idea of applying electric action to the organ is as old as

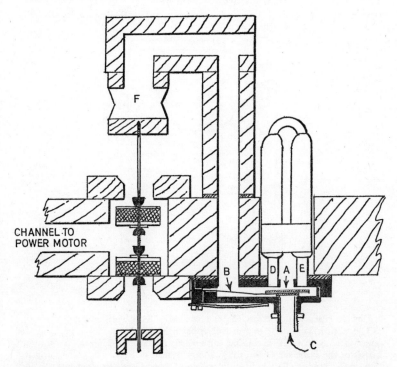

6. An electro-pneumatic-primary action with the electro-magnet arranged slightly differently from that of Figure 5, but showing it in greater detail. The disc-valve armature (A), through the pressure of its spring (B) seals the escape windway (C) from the outer atmosphere. When the poles of the electro-magnet (D) (E) are energized, the disc-valve armature is drawn towards them, opening the windway and enabling the pressure air in the primary motor (F) to exhaust into the outer atmosphere.

the electro-magnet itself, but it does not seem to have been used successfully until about 1866 (at Salon near Marseilles by C. S. Barker, who used an idea of Dr Albert Peschard). Despite much useful pioneer work on the Continent and by Robert Hope-Jones in Britain, it caught on slowly and did not become standard practice with leading British organ makers until the 1920s.

Modern electro-pneumatic action is of two main types. Figures 5 and 6 show the type used with traditional 'slider chests' in which all the pipes belonging to a particular note are winded by one pallet. Figure 7 shows a type used with 'sliderless

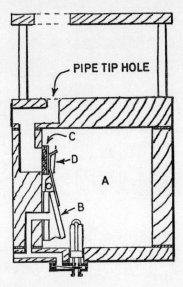

PIPE TIP HOLE

7. Electro-pneumatic action, slider-less chest, 'Roosevelt' system.
The action is shown in the 'off' position. The windchest (A) and the pneumatic motor (B) are filled with pressurized air. The electro-magnet works in the same way as in the primary action of Figure 6, exhausting the pneumatic motor (B) which collapses and opens the attached pallet-valve (C) against the tension of its spring (D). When the magnet is de-energized the series of events is reversed.

chests' in which each pipe is separately winded and may be wired by the organ builder to any selected key.* There is also 'direct electric' action (Figure 8), a cheaper and on the whole less efficient form of action for sliderless chests.

Although the speed of electricity is virtually instantaneous it does not follow that electro-pneumatic action will necessarily

*Sliderless chests are used where it is convenient to place pipes away from the main slider chests; also in organs built on the 'extension' or 'unit' system, which is explained on page 63.

give instantaneous response. The speed of operation is determined by the efficiency of the pneumatic part of the mechanism. Unless this is of first-rate quality, response tends to be sluggish, particularly in the bass where the pallets are large and the work is heavy. With electro-pneumatic action, no less than with older types, only the best can give satisfactory musical results.

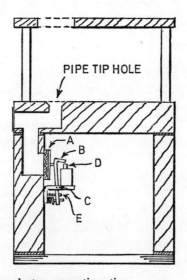

8. Direct electric or electro-magnetic action.
 This contains no pneumatic mechanism. The pallet-valve (A) is attached to a metal lever (B) pivoted at (C). When the electroc-magnet is energized the tip of the lever is drawn across the inclined tip of the magnet pole (D) against the tension of the coil spring (E), pulling the pallet-valve open.

Electric actions enable the console to be detached any distance from the rest of the organ—an obvious advantage where this is awkwardly placed. But since sound takes time to travel, detachment beyond thirty feet (less in reverberant buildings) causes a noticeable acoustic time-lag which, especially if added to any mechanical time-lag, is very disturbing to the player. There is then little feeling of contact with the source of sound and sensitive playing is virtually impossible. Nevertheless, a good electro-pneumatic action combined with the right kind of pipework, and a console near the instrument, can be of irreproachable response; though it cannot, by its very nature, match up to the intimacy of tracker.

The touch of organs with electric action is usually of the spring type; the key is held against the pressure of a spring which returns it to rest. Weight of touch can be adjusted by the organ builder, but there is no top resistance. Artificial top resistance, giving something of a tracker feel, is sometimes provided by means of toggle springs.

Combined Actions

Two or more different actions are sometimes combined in a single instrument. An old organ with tracker manual action may have tubular-pneumatic pedal action. Pneumatic-lever was usually applied only to the heavier great organ, tracker being used elsewhere. Tracker and electric actions have recently been successfully combined. This is particularly advantageous where the tonal resources of an old tracker organ have to be extended and new pipes and windchests cannot be accommodated in an existing layout.

Nowadays pneumatic-lever and tubular-pneumatic actions are obsolete; but they survive in many old organs. For many years tracker action was also thought to be obsolete, largely through misapplication and a misunderstanding of its virtues. In the second half of the twentieth century its merits are again recognized by leading organists and makers. Most new or re-built British organs have some form of electric action, or tracker, according to circumstances.

II

How Organ Tone is Produced

The Harmonic Series

Having grasped the general principles of organ construction we can now look to the pipes themselves and consider how organ tone is produced, before considering how it is compounded into choruses. To do this it is first necessary to relate a few elementary acoustical facts.

An elastic body, such as a stretched string or a colum of air in an organ pipe, has a natural period of free vibration. The frequency of these vibrations (disregarding certain subjective considerations) determines the pitch of the musical note produced by the body—the faster the frequency, the higher the note. The length of an organ pipe or string needed to yield a given note is halved (other things being equal) every octave above, but the frequency is doubled. Thus, given that an open-end pipe about 8 ft long sounds CC* with a frequency of 64 cycles per second, a 4 ft pipe sounds C (128 c.p.s.), a 2 ft pipe c^1 (256 c.p.s.) and so on. By the same rule a pipe $2\frac{2}{3}$ ft long sounds G (192 c.p.s.).

A stretched string or an air column of an organ pipe does not merely vibrate as a whole. It also vibrates simultaneously in sections measurable as fractions ($\frac{1}{2}$, $\frac{1}{3}$, $\frac{1}{4}$, $\frac{1}{5}$, $\frac{1}{6}$, etc) of its length, which consequently produce frequencies of 2, 3, 4, 5, 6 etc, times that of the body as a whole. Each of these frequencies produces its own note, an 'overtone' or 'upper partial'. These,

* See notation and pitch table p. 33.

19

together with the note of the whole length of the body, the 'fundamental', fall into a series known as the 'harmonic series'. If the fundamental is 8 ft CC, the bottom note of the modern organ keyboard, the first 16 notes of the series are:

Numbering of the harmonic series   1 2 3   4   5 6 7 8 9 10 11 12 13 14 15 16

Of these, only the fundamental (No. 1) and its octaves (Nos. 2, 4, 8 and 16) are in tune with our equal-tempered keyboard scale; the fifths (Nos. 3, 6 and 12) are slightly out of tune with it and the remaining harmonics more so.

The number of harmonics that are present in a musical sound, and their relative strengths is the principal, though by no means the only factor determining its tone quality. A brilliant tone—such as that of a trumpet or violin—is rich in harmonics. At the other extreme is the dull, round tone of a tuning fork consisting of pure fundamental with no harmonics at all; and there are countless intermediary stages.

The natural harmonic series is a phenomenon of tremendous importance in organ design. Not only is it the stuff of which the tone colours of individual stops are made; it also underlies the art of creating synthetic tone colours by blending several stops of various pitches, and welding several stops into a chorus. These are matters which we will come to shortly.

There are two types of organ pipe: 'flue' or 'labial', and 'reed' or 'lingual'. Flue pipes produce sound in the same manner as an orchestral flute or piccolo, through an air column excited into vibration by an edge or lip tone. In reed pipes the sound is produced as in an orchestral clarinet or oboe—by an air column that qualifies the sound of a vibrating reed. All organ pipes, in fact, are coupled systems of tone production in which the sound is generated by two systems, neither of which can function without interference from the other. This is explained in more detail below.

Flue Pipes

Flue pipes are classified 'open' or 'stopped' according to whether the top ends are open or closed to the atmosphere. Examples of both kinds are shown diagramatically in Figures 9 and 10.

The method of tone production is as follows. Wind enters the foothole and is transformed by the narrow slit of the flue into a thin stream of air which is directed against the edge of the upper lip. As the air-stream meets the lip it breaks into a series of little whirlwinds or vortices. The frequency at which these impinge

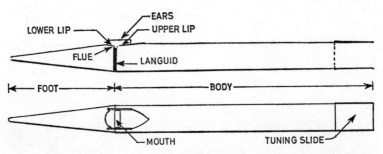

9. Diagram of an open metal flue pipe. Tuning is effected by upward or downward movements of the loose-fitting tuning slide, lengthening or shortening the vibrating air column in the pipe body.

upon the lip produces a more or less musical note with overtones known as an 'edge tone'. Simultaneously the air column in the pipe body is set in motion and generates a much stronger note with its own overtones. Although the stronger partner predominates, the overtones of the edge tone influence those of the air column and consequently the composite tone of the whole pipe. The locking together of the two systems in an agreeable balance is part of the pipe voicer's technique.

What are the main factors which determine the tone of a flue pipe? First of all there is the body shape. For reasons which we need not go into here, an open pipe vibrates in all its sections and consequently produces a complete series of harmonics. But in a fully-stopped pipe the alternate sections vibrate and only odd-numbered harmonics are produced. For this reason, the characteristic tone quality yielded by open and stopped pipes is entirely different (though much variety is obtainable within each type by other means). Moreover, a stopped pipe yields a note an octave lower in pitch than an open pipe of approximately equivalent length. More tonal variety can be obtained by modifying the body shape of each type so as to introduce

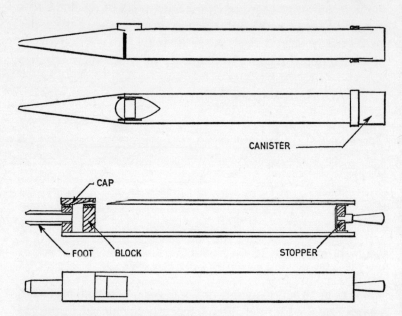

10. Diagram of stopped flue pipes: (top) metal with canister stopper; (bottom) wood with ordinary stopper. Tuning is effected by moving the canister or the stopper upwards or downwards, lengthening or shortening the vibrating air column in the body.

harmonic characteristics of the other. If an open metal pipe is made *partly* stopped by tapering the body inwards, the odd-numbered harmonics are strengthened at the expense of the even-numbered, and the tone assumes a hybrid character. Similarly, if an open 'chimney' is inserted in the stopper of a stopped pipe, or if the stopper is pierced, weak even-numbered harmonics appear and the result is another hybrid tone, different from that obtained from the tapered construction. Stops constructed in this way are said to be 'half-stopped' or 'half-covered'. The application of these shapes to different kinds of stops is illustrated in Plate I.

Other important features that govern the tone of flue pipes are:

Scale: the width of the pipe body*
Width and height (or 'cut up') of the mouth
Bevel of the languid edge and thickness of the upper lip
Small movements of upper and lower lips, languid and ears
'Nicking' the languid and lower lip of a metal pipe, or 'grooving' the block of a wooden one
Pressure of wind (controlled by weighting the reservoir)
Amount of wind (governed by the size of the foothole)
Material of which the pipes are made

The scale determines the breadth of tone and the general character of the stop. Wide scales encourage fullness of tone at the expense of harmonic development. With narrow scales the tone tends to be rich in overtones (that is, brighter) but softer and with less body. A wide, low mouth yields a louder and brighter tone than a narrow one. A relatively high mouth eliminates some of the acute overtones and makes the tone quality duller.

The scale of an organ pipe, unlike its body length, does not halve at every octave (12 notes) of the compass. If it did the trebles would be intolerably weak and thin in relation to the bass. For this reason the scale of flue pipes is made to halve every seventeenth or eighteenth pipe, never lower, and sometimes as high as the twentieth or twenty-second pipe, depending on the amount of treble fullness desired.

The attack of an organ pipe, like the initial 'chiff' of an orchestral flute or the 'bite' of a violin bow as it attacks the

* In cylindrical pipes the scale is measured in terms of the diameter; in rectangular ones in terms of the area of the pipe top. In tapered pipes the material scale measurements are the top and bottom diameter and the ratios of the taper.

string, contributes more to its individual tone character than any other single factor. Remove the attack from an orchestral trumpet, violin or oboe and the differences between them are much harder to identify. Flue pipe attack is controlled by very small adjustments of the lips and languid (for instance, by pushing in or pulling out the upper lip a fraction of an inch) and by 'nicking'—cutting small notches in the lower lip and the languid of a metal pipe or grooves in the bluck of a wooden one. Depending on the depth and spacing of the notches or grooves, this treatment either modifies or eliminates the 'chiffing' effect of initiation tones which occur during the fraction of a second when the wind-pressure is building up in the pipe foot. If it is overdone (as it often was in the 'romantic' organs of the late nineteenth and early twentieth centuries) the speech tends to be slow and unclear. Modern 'classical' voicing has returned to seventeenth- and eighteenth-century methods. Nicking is either minimized or completely avoided and initiation tones are controlled by careful lip and languid adjustments. The object of this is to give the pipes a quick, clean attack, so that they are clear and responsive in musical use, particularly in conjunction with tracker action.*

The pressure and quantity of wind on which a stop is voiced both contribute to the tonal character. Wind-pressure is measured by a wind-gauge in inches of water. The effect of these features on organ tone is a very complex matter. All that need be said here is that for fluework, low wind-pressures—that is, not exceeding $3\frac{1}{2}$ in—and wide footholes are generally preferred because they produce a natural, unforced singing

---

* At this stage an attempt must be made to define the terms 'classical' and 'romantic' in the sense that they are commonly applied to organs. They are broad terms used to denote opposed conceptions of the instrument, and have only the vaguest associations with classical and romantic music as such. A 'romantic' organ is one designed, in accordance with nineteenth- and early twentieth-century practice, for the purpose of emulating, to some extent, the dynamic expression peculiar to the orchestra. A 'classical' organ is one designed in accordance with the methods of the seventeenth- and eighteenth-century French and German organ makers, who never attempted to make the organ behave like anything but an organ. All this should become clear later.

tone combined with good attack. Here again, modern taste is reverting to the practice of the seventeenth and eighteenth centuries.

Reed Pipes

The construction of a reed pipe is shown in Figure 11. Clearly this is considerably more involved than a flue pipe, there being at least eight separate components.

When the wind enters the boothole it causes the brass reed to vibrate against the opening of the shallot. Beyond this stands a column of air in the resonator or tube, which is also set in vibration. The reed itself produces many dissonant overtones that are disagreeable to the ear, in addition to the principal note of its free vibrations. But the resonator is constructed so that its air-column reinforces only the consonant overtones, and the result is a rich, pleasing musical sound.

As with the flue pipe, the shape of the reed pipe resonator is a material factor in determining the tone quality. A conical (strictly, an *inverted* conical) resonator reinforces the complete harmonic series. A cylindrical resonator reinforces only the odd-numbered harmonics. Unlike the flue pipe, however, the length of the resonator (the air-column) may be varied for tonal reasons without affecting the pitch. This is because in the flue pipe, as we have seen, the body length must be exactly that needed to yield the natural frequency of its note. But since the main tone producer of the reed pipe is the reed (whose tones the resonator air-column only serves to colour and amplify) the natural frequencies of reed and resonator need not be the same, indeed for purposes of obtaining varied stops they are often deliberately made different. Depending on the desired tone quality, resonators may be either full length (i.e., having about the same natural frequency as the reed); or fractional length (i.e., half, quarter or one-eighth); or 'harmonic' (i.e., double or triple length). Plate I illustrates the application of some of these methods to different kinds of reed stops.

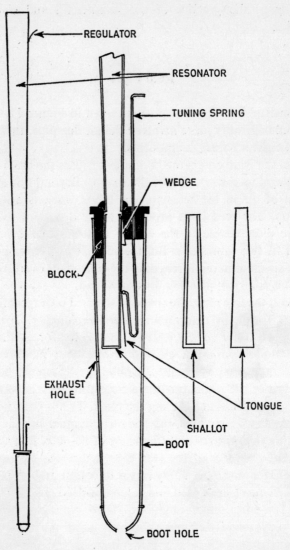

REGULATOR

RESONATOR

TUNING SPRING

WEDGE

BLOCK

EXHAUST HOLE

TONGUE

SHALLOT

BOOT

BOOT HOLE

11. Components of a reed pipe. The pipe is tuned in two ways: by small movements of the tuning spring, varying the vibrating length of the tongue; and by using the 'regulator', a slot cut near to top of the resonator and bent outwards, to vary the length of the vibrating air column.

26

II. Four manual and pedal drawstop console, Coventry Cathedral, Harrison & Harrison Ltd, 1962. Note the slight curvature of the stop jambs and the two centrally placed swell pedals, (L) swell organ, (R) solo organ.

Other important factors which influence the tone and power
of reed pipes are:

Thickness, length, shape and curve of the tongue, and whether
it is 'weighted'
Shape of the shallot and its opening
Scale: diameter of the resonator at the top and bottom
Wind pressure and size of the boothole
Material of which the resonator is made

The ratio adopted for the halving of reed-pipe scales varies
greatly for different types of reed and individual voicing practice.
But generally the ratio is much higher than that normally
applied to flue pipes.

Reed pipes constructed so that the natural frequencies of the
reed and tube do not differ greatly are said to be voiced 'at
resonance'. The rich, pleasing tones of trumpets made by
Father Willis are produced in this manner, and this type of tone
quality has come to be regarded as 'normal' to British ears. But
if the tube is slightly lengthened in relation to the reed, the tone
becomes stifled or 'close' and more horn-like in quality. Shortening the tube makes the tone 'free', that is, more brilliant.
A completely open shallot enables the reed to convey all
its harmonics to the tube, producing very brilliant tone.
A small, constricted opening limits the transmission of harmonics and encourages a smoother, more constricted kind of
tone.

Excellent quick-speaking trumpet tone is obtainable on the
low wind-pressure suitable for fluework. But when greater
power is desired, higher pressures (from about 7 in upwards)
are needed to give the tongue sufficient amplification of movement; and it is then necessary to dampen the ardour of the
basses by affixing small brass or felt weights to the free ends of
the tongues. The technique of heavy-pressure reed voicing dates
back rather more than a century. The difficulty is that heavy-
pressure reeds, often arresting in themselves, tend to obscure the
flue-work. Because of this, modern taste has come to prefer
the older, low-pressure reed which, although lacking the

sophistication of later stops, does not obliterate the fluework and has wider general utility.

Materials from which Organ Pipes are Made

It is a well known fact in the construction of musical instruments that some materials will contribute towards a better quality of tone than others. This also applies to organ pipes. Centuries of experience have shown that the best pipe metal is a lead-tin alloy, and the higher the proportion of tin the brighter and clearer the tone. For economy, large bass flue pipes are often made of zinc (occasionally of copper) but with lead-tin alloy mouths. For wooden flue pipes, oak, mahogany, pine or pear give good tone. Wooden pipes are generally thought to yield a darker, warmer and more mellow tone than metal ones. An explanation of these differences is that each kind of pipe material produces its own free vibrations, known as the 'formant'. The formant, which will vary according to the kind and quality of material, is reinforced by resonance with the vibrations of the air-column, and makes its own contributions to the composite tone quality of the pipe.

Tonal Families

The variety of organ stops obtainable by the voicing methods just outlined is immense; but they fall into four tonal families which the student should learn to recognize. The basis of this classification is purely aural. Organ stops can also be classified according to pipe construction. However, the author believes that an aural classification is the only practicable one for the reader who is just beginning to understand the instrument.

The first aural distinction must be between flues and reeds. Because of the different systems of tone production, the attack and general character of each type is so distinctive that there will be no difficulty in distinguishing between them. Flue stops fall into three sub-divisions: foundation, flute and string; but within each of these will be found a few stops of hybrid tone quality which partake something of the general character of another group. Reeds, too, can be sub-grouped according to whether they are intended primarily for chorus or solo use. But again some overlapping is inevitable, since some primarily solo reeds can be used effectively in chorus.

This may seem very complicated, but it is not so difficult as may first appear. Unfortunately, tonal qualities cannot be described adequately in words, and a short experimental period at the keyboard of a reasonably equipped organ will help to put the following explanation of the four tonal families of the organ —foundation, flute, string and reed—into perspective. Much can be learned, too, by listening carefully to organ recitals and gramophone recordings of organ music. From this stage on, it is suggested that the Glossary of Organ Stops in Part III should be consulted when unfamiliar stop names are encountered.

(1) *Foundation*

All these stops have open pipes, usually of metal. The main foundation stops are the diapasons (open diapason, principal), of which the main flue choruses of the organ are constructed. Diapason tone has a strong fundamental with fairly generous harmonic development, and is instantly recognizable as unique organ tone. Flute, string and reed stops have some affinity with corresponding orchestral instruments; but diapason tone is the inimitable sound of the organ as such. The Spitzflöte and Gemshorn are often voiced so brightly that they may be regarded as belonging to the foundation class rather than the flutes. Diminutive stops of very quiet diapason quality (dulciana, salicional) should strictly be included in the foundation class, since they are, in effect, miniature open diapasons.

(2) *Flute*

Stops in this group are so classified because of their 'fluty' tone—rounder *timbres* and larger scales than foundation or string stops. Individual flute stops are distinguishable according

29

to whether they are open, stopped, or half-stopped. Open flutes (clarabella, open flute, Hohlflöte, Waldflöte) have a characteristically 'pure' tone with a bold fundamental and octave but weak upper harmonics. Stopped flutes (stopped diapason, bourdon, Lieblich Gedeckt) have strong odd-numbered harmonics and a perky but mellow tone. The half-stopped registers (Rohrflöte, Koppel, Spitzflöte) combine something of the characteristics of both the other kinds, and by an interlamination of even-numbered harmonics achieve an even more colourful character. In some of their manifestations the Spitzflöte and Gemshorn can be so rich in harmonics that they yield a bright flute-string quality which, despite their grouping with the flutes, makes them more at home among the foundation stops. They are among the indefinable hybrid stops mentioned above.

(3) *String*

String stops have a bright and warm tonality suggestive of bowed string instruments. Intense *timbres* of this kind—a rich complement of harmonics and comparatively weak fundamental—are produced by open pipes, usually of metal, but of narrower scale than is customary for diapasons and flutes. There are two main kinds:

(a) 'Organ-type' Strings;
   of broad, gentle quality—aeoline, viola da gamba, violone.

(b) 'Orchestral-type' Strings:
   voiced to emulate so far as possible the tone of modern orchestral strings. These are pungent, keen and intense, and of very narrow scale—viole d'orchestre, viole sourdine.

Undulating stops (see Voix céleste in the Glossary, page 179) are usually of string tone. A few hybrid stops have a diapason-string sonority—violin diapason, geigen diapason, horn diapason.

(4) *Reed*

Any attempt at a strict classification of reed stops would involve

several confusing sub-divisions. Three main groups must
suffice.

(a) Chorus Reeds:
These are voiced primarily to form part of a reed chorus, or
to blend with a flue chorus. All have conical reasonators.
The tone quality is reminiscent of orchestral brass (with an
intense fundamental and a brilliant superstructure of harmonics)—trombone, trumpet, tromba, posaune, tuba.

(b) Organ-type Solo or Special Reeds:
Highly individualized stops of varied construction. Although
based on the sounds of old and modern musical instruments
(from which their names are derived) they are in no sense
meant to be faithful imitations of such instruments, and are
part of the traditional palette of 'true' organ tones. The types
are too varied to be described here, and the reader is referred
to the Glossary—oboe, fagotto, Krummhorn, Schalmai,
Regal, Dulcian. The vox humana is also proper to this group.

(c) Orchestral Imitations:
Special solo stops voiced in deliberate imitation of modern
orchestral wind instruments—orchestral oboe, clarinet, cor
anglais, French horn, orchestral trumpet. The static nature
of organ tone makes it impossible for such stops to be more
than clever suggestions of the real thing.

We have now outlined the layout and workings of the organ,
the production of sound in individual stops, and the grouping
of these stops into families. But an organ is more than a
capricious collection of beautifully voiced stops. In order that
it may serve a practical musical purpose, the stops must be
disposed in accordance with an intelligent tonal design: but
above all, the major stops must be designed so as to combine
into a cohesive and musically satisfying tonal ensemble. In
other words they must become a *chorus*. The next section of
this book will explain how this is done.

III

Chorus Structure

The Pitch of Organ Stops

Organ choruses are constructed, not by the multiplication of stops of unison pitch (i.e., the same pitch as the corresponding note on the pianoforte or as sung by the human voice), but by adding to a single unison other stops sounding the octave, the super-octave and other consonant intervals of the harmonic series. Other musical instruments obtain increases of loudness and brilliance by a natural intensification of harmonics. But in the organ, whose stops can sound only at a pre-determined level, this can only be done by adding the appropriate harmonics artifically.

A chorus which is both powerful and brilliant cannot be obtained by multiplying unison stops. The reason for this is inherent in the nature of sound. A doubling of intensity at any particular level only produces an increase of about 3 phons or units of loudness. For example: 5+5 phons=8 phons; 100+100 phons=103 phons. Thus, the louder a particular stop is, the greater is the amount of unison tone that must be added to it to obtain a just perceptible increase of loudness. Greatly increased power at unison level, therefore, can only be obtained by adding more unison stops of ever-increasing loudness, to which there are practical as well as musical limits. There are also practical limits to the degree of natural harmonic brilliance obtainable from single stops. But if a unison stop is supplemented at octave pitch by another stop of similar output, the

The Pitch of Organ Stops

NOTATION AND PITCH TABLE

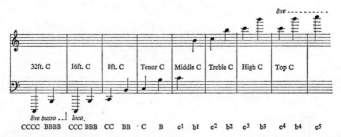

The above table shows organ builders' pitch notation, which is used throughout this book. The more convenient Helmholtz pitch notation, to which organ builders have yet to be converted, refers to organ builders' CC, C, c^1, c^2 etc. as C, c, c′, c″ etc. Organ builders sometimes refer to B instead of B♭ and ♮ instead of B. Hence B A C H = B♭ A C B. Historically in England the octave was often regarded as beginning at G. Thus the diatonic sequence from the G below 16 ft C was: GGG to FFF sharp, GG to FF sharp, G etc. The latter G, equivalent to the violin G string, was called 'fiddle G'.

---

power is effectively doubled and much brilliance is added besides. It was discovered quite early in the development of the organ that this is the only practicable method of constructing a brilliant and telling chorus—the early organ builders having very cleverly anticipated the findings of the nineteenth-century physicist Helmholtz* by at least three centuries.

Stops are made, therefore, to sound at many pitches other than the unison. The pitch of a stop is denoted on the stop-knob or stop-switch by the length in feet of its longest pipe. For this purpose, the actual differences between the length of pipes of various kinds of construction are disregarded. It is assumed that CC (the lowest note of the modern manual keyboard) equals 8 ft: the approximate speaking length of an open flue pipe required to produce that note. As explained earlier, the speaking lengths of pipes halve at every octave

* Herman Ludwig Ferdinand von Helmholtz (1821–1894), physiologist and physicist. His *Die Lehre dem Tonempfindung* (1862), translated by A. J. Ellis as *On the Sensations of Tone as a Physiological Basis for the Theory of Music* is the basis of modern theories of musical acoustics.

PITCHES OF STOPS

MANUALS Pitch length shown on stop label feet	MANUALS Note sounded at CC key†	Description of Pitch	PEDALS Pitch length shown on stop label feet	PEDALS Note sounded at CCC key†
1	c^2	Twenty-second	2	c^1
$1\frac{1}{7}$	b flat^1	Flat twenty-first (septieme)	* $2\frac{2}{7}$	B flat
$1\frac{1}{3}$	g^1	Nineteenth (larigot)	$2\frac{2}{3}$	G
$1\frac{3}{5}$	e^1	Seventeenth (tierce)	* $3\frac{1}{5}$	E
2	c^1	Fifteenth (superoctave)	4	C
* $2\frac{2}{7}$	B flat	Flat fourteenth (septieme)	* $4\frac{4}{7}$	BB flat
$2\frac{2}{3}$	G	Twelfth (octave quint)	$5\frac{1}{3}$	GG
* $3\frac{1}{5}$	E	Tenth (gross tierce)	* $6\frac{2}{5}$	EE
4	C	Octave	8	CC
$5\frac{1}{3}$	GG	Quint	$10\frac{2}{3}$	GGG
8	CC	Unison	16	CCC
* $10\frac{2}{3}$	GGG	Sub-quint	* $21\frac{1}{3}$	GGGG
16	CCC	Sub-unison (double)	32	CCCC
* 32	CCCC	—	* 64	CCCCC

* stops of these pitches are found only in very large or unusual organs.

† As with the harmonic series, only the octaves are in tune with the equal-tempered scale, see p. 20.

34

above and diminish proportionately in between. Since, therefore, CC equals 8 ft: C equals 4 ft, G equals $2\frac{2}{3}$ ft, c^1 equals 2 ft, e^1 equals $1\frac{3}{5}$ ft, and so on. Thus, a manual stop in which CC sounds as written (the same pitch as the corresponding note on the pianoforte or as sung by the human voice), is said to be of 8 ft 'unison' or pitch. A stop sounding the octave above unison is said to be of 4 ft pitch; the twelfth above is $2\frac{2}{3}$ ft pitch; the superoctave or fifteenth above is 2 ft pitch; the seventeenth above is $1\frac{3}{5}$ ft pitch; and so on. Similarly, a stop sounding an octave below unison is 16 ft pitch. Manual 16 ft stops are called 'doubles'.

The pitch of the pedal organ is an octave lower than the manual pitch, so that 32 ft is regarded as the 'double' pitch, 16 ft as the unison, 8 ft as the octave, and so on.

An examination of the table opposite in conjunction with the notation and pitch table on page 33 will show the actual notes sounded by stops of various pitches on manuals and pedals. It will be seen that it is possible for stops to be available in at least eighteen different pitches from 64 ft to 1 ft. Some of these (indicated by an asterisk) are found only in unusual or very large organs, but they are included for completeness. Stops that sound pitches other than the unison or its octaves ($5\frac{1}{3}$ ft, $3\frac{1}{5}$ ft, $2\frac{2}{3}$ ft, etc) are called, in strict terminology, 'mutation' stops.* Flue stops may appear in all available pitches; but reed stops rarely appear above 4 ft pitch or in the form of mutations.

Single-rank stops of higher pitches than 1 ft (e.g., $\frac{1}{3}$ ft or $\frac{1}{2}$ ft) are so unusual that for practical purposes they may be disregarded. Nevertheless, ranks of pipes sounding pitches above 1 ft are commonly used in choruses. These do not draw separately but are grouped in stops sounding two, three or more pipes to each note. These are known as 'compound stops' or 'mixtures', and are denoted by various names, such as mixture, furniture (or fourniture), cymbale, harmonics and sesquialtera,

---

* Because they change the note which is played. The term is often loosely used, however, to denote any stop above 4 ft pitch.

followed by the number of ranks they contain—usually in Roman numerals.* Stops of pitches above unison are known generally as 'upperwork'.

The Organ Specification

The foregoing account of the pitches of organ stops will set the reader well on the way to appreciating the stop-list or 'specification' of an organ. A specification is mainly a list of the stops an organ contains, set out under the various departments in order of pitch, flues first, reeds second.

For instance, the specification of the imaginary small organ of Figure 1 would be set out thus—like many small organs, it has no reeds:

TYPICAL SMALL ORGAN

GREAT ORGAN			SWELL ORGAN		
1.	Stopped diapason	8 ft	4.	Rohrflöte	8 ft
2.	Principal	4	5.	Spitzflöte	4
3.	Fifteenth	2	6.	Mixture	III ranks

PEDAL ORGAN			COUPLERS
7.	Bourdon	16 ft	Great to pedal
8.	Principal	8	Swell to pedal
9.	Gemshorn	4	Swell to great

The paper specification can give a good impression of the musical scope of an organ provided the style of the maker is known. A soundly designed and balanced specification is the first requisite of a good organ.

Armed with this knowledge we can now consider the chorus structure of the organ. Choruses can be constructed from each of the four main stop families. But when a well designed full organ is heard in all its majesty and brilliance, two particular

* Some of these terms have strict meanings, but like much organ-stop nomenclature, they are often used imprecisely. The reader is referred to the Glossary of Organ Stops, Part III, p. 161.

choruses will predominate—a *flue chorus* of open diapason or principal stops and a *reed chorus* of stops of the trumpet class. These must be considered separately.

The Diapason or Principal Chorus

Each organ division may have its own diapason chorus, but the predominant one always appears on the great organ, and this forms the basic chorus structure of the instrument.

A 'pure' diapason chorus consists solely of a blend of octaves and fifths, a coalescent spread of sound extending from unison, even sub-unison, pitch to high-pitched mixtures. Third-sounding ranks (tierces) strictly form no part of this structure because they add thickness and reediness to the pure tone that soon becomes wearisome. But they are often made available separately for special colouring effects.

During all the best periods of organ building, diapason choruses have been constructed of ranks of more or less equal volume (the fifths being perhaps slightly softer than the octaves), experience having shown that this treatment spreads the acoustic energy as widely as possible, and produces the most satisfactory musical results.

The following selection of stops from an imaginary great organ—a complete diapason chorus—will help to illustrate the principle upon which a traditional diapason chorus is constructed:

1. Open diapason   8 ft
2. Principal (or octave)   4
3. Twelfth (or octave quint) $2\frac{2}{3}$
4. Fifteenth (or super-octave)   2
5. Mixture $1\frac{1}{3}'-1'-\frac{2}{3}'-\frac{1}{2}'$ IV ranks

The practical limits on the length of an open flue pipe are 32 ft at one end and about half-an-inch at the other. Since the 8 ft, 4 ft, $2\frac{2}{3}$ ft and 2 ft stops of this chorus fall well within these limits, they run without interruption from bottom to top of the

37

compass. The mixture, however, consists of small pipes which cannot feasibly be carried up to the top of the keyboard. It is necessary, therefore, to return or 'break' the smallest pipe back to a lower-pitched one at appropriate stages of the compass. The pitches of the ranks at the various stages and the way the breaks are contrived are known as the 'composition' of the mixture.

Our hypothetical mixture follows a conventional pattern. Its composition, set out below, may be expressed in two ways: in terms of pitch lengths (A), or of intervals from the unison (B). The latter method is more frequently used and will be followed throughout this book, but the reader ought to be familiar with both.

	A					B			
	I	II	III	IV		I	II	III	IV
CC to BB=	$1\frac{1}{3}'$	$1'$	$\frac{2}{3}'$	$\frac{1}{2}'$	CC to BB=	19	22	26	29
C to B=	$2'$	$1\frac{1}{3}'$	$1'$	$\frac{2}{3}'$	C to B=	15	19	22	26
c^1 to b^1=	$2\frac{2}{3}'$	$2'$	$1\frac{1}{3}'$	$1'$	c^1 to b^1=	12	15	19	22
c^2 to b^2=	$4'$	$2\frac{2}{3}'$	$2'$	$1\frac{1}{3}'$	c^2 to b^2=	8	12	15	19
c^3 to top=	$8'$	$4'$	$2\frac{2}{3}'$	$2'$	c^3 to top=	1	8	12	15

The impracticability of carrying very small pipes up to the top of the keyboard is by no means the only reason for mixture breaks. They also serve an important musical purpose. To illustrate this, let us see what happens in the various parts of the five-octave compass of the great organ (CC to c^4) when all the five chorus stops are drawn. Again, this is expressed in terms of intervals from the unison but, for ease of understanding, the position at CC is first set out in terms of musical notation:

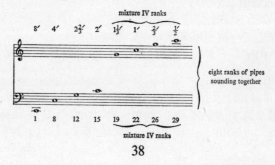

The Diapason or Principal Chorus

CC to BB = 1	8	12	15	**19**	**22**	**26**	**29**
C to B = 1	8	12	15	**15**	**19**	**22**	**26**
c¹ to b¹ = 1	8	12	**12**	15	**15**	**19**	**22**
c² to b² = 1	8	**8**	**12**	12	**15**	15	**19**
c³ to top = 1	**1**	8	**8**	12	**12**	15	**15**

The four mixture ranks are shown in bold type to distinguish them from the independent 8 ft, 4 ft, 2⅔ ft and 2 ft ranks.

It can be seen that the effect of the mixture breaks is to make the composition of the entire chorus change at each octave of the compass. As the compass rises, the high-pitched ranks in the bass are gradually replaced by lower-pitched ones until, in the top octave, the independent ranks are completely doubled. In this way the breaks help to give the full chorus a musical balance which is otherwise unobtainable—by giving definition to the bass, brilliance to the middle register and solidity to the trebles. This function of mixtures is especially important for the performance of polyphonic music, where clarity of inner parts and a melodic treble line are essential.

A mixture of the kind just described is known as a 'ripieno' or 'filling-up' mixture. But this is not the sole function of mixtures. There are, for example, 'sharp mixtures' and 'cimbels' composed of even higher-pitched ranks, and designed to give brilliance and a sense of climax to a chorus rather than fullness. Not all mixture breaks occur on a C. Breaks are often arranged to occur on other notes according to the desired result, and to avoid the noticeable effect of two or more mixtures breaking on the same note.

The importance of mixtures cannot be overstressed. If they are voiced too stridently or are allowed to get out of tune they are naturally unbearable, and have been much misunderstood for these reasons. But properly designed mixtures are the life-blood of the organ. Not only do they fill out and clarify the chorus in the manner just explained. They also spread the acoustic energy so as to give an impression of power without loudness. They produce liveliness of tone through the clash of their perfect intervals and resultant tones with the notes of the tempered scale.* And their harmonic superstructure helps to weld the diapason and reed choruses into a cohesive mass of tone.

The words of the great Victorian organist, W. T. Best, are worth quoting. He wrote in 1881: 'It is particularly necessary to stress the extreme importance of mixture work, artistically tempered and of melodious sonority. No other legitimate means exist, nor can ever exist, of adding harmonious power to an organ'.

The Reed Chorus

The construction of a reed chorus can be explained very briefly. It consists of a set of trumpet-quality chorus reeds in unison, octave and sub-octave pitches.

The blaze of natural harmonics produced by chorus reeds and the unfeasibility of making very small reed pipes rule out reed upperwork on both musical and practical grounds. Chorus reeds do not, therefore, normally appear above 4 ft pitch, although there are a few freakish exceptions. Any upward extension of the reed chorus must be provided by flue upperwork—either that of the diapason chorus doing double duty, or a separate, brightly-voiced mixture specially designed to crown the trumpet sub-structure and weld the whole into a scintillating mass of tone.

A reed chorus complete with its own upperwork can be specified thus:

Double Trumpet   16 ft
Trumpet   8
Clarion   4
Mixture (12 15 19 22 26 29) VI ranks

Reed choruses of various kinds appear in all divisions of large

* Resultant tones are faint notes resulting from the sounding of two notes simultaneously; e.g., an interval of a fifth produces a resultant an octave below the lower note.

organs. But in the same way that the great organ is the home of the main diapason chorus, so in organs of moderate size the swell organ is the home of the main reed chorus, in the sense that complete provision is properly made for it there before other reed choruses are introduced in the tonal scheme.

The Flute Chorus and Solo Mutations

In addition to the main diapason and reed choruses a well designed organ will contain in one or more of its divisions a chorus of flutes including some 'solo' mutations. For example:

Gedeckt	8 ft
Rohrflöte	4
*Nasard (or Nazard)	$2\frac{2}{3}$
Blockflöte	2
*Tierce	$1\frac{3}{5}$
*Larigot	$1\frac{1}{3}$
Sifflöte	1

The solo mutations are indicated by an asterisk.

A solo mutation is flute-toned—as distinct from a chorus mutation which is diapason-toned—and designed primarily for synthetic tone-building. Just as natural harmonics combine to form the characteristic tone-colours of individual stops, so the artificial harmonics of solo mutations can be selected to form distinctive compound tone-colours. These sonorities are entirely characteristic of the organ and can be obtained in no other way. The individual pitches lose their identity in the tone colour they create.

A few examples will be given. Drawn with a neutral-toned 8 ft stop, the nasard colours the basic tone by adding a somewhat nasal timbre, which seems to merit the name. The addition of the tierce makes the tone reedy and clarinet-like. Substitution of a string stop for the neutral 8 ft pitch synthesizes a tone-colour not unlike an oboe. The larigot $1\frac{1}{3}$ ft adds a perky brightness to whatever is drawn with it; and there are many other possibilities.

Solo mutations also appear in the form of compound stops, for instance, the 'cornet' and the 'sesquialtera'. In its complete form the cornet consists of five wide-scale ranks: a stopped 8 ft, and open metal 4 ft, $2\frac{2}{3}$ ft, 2 ft and $1\frac{3}{5}$ ft, the combined effect of which is a full, reed-like sonority. The sesquialtera consists of two ranks, $2\frac{2}{3}$ ft and $1\frac{3}{5}$ ft. Both these stops can be used in solos, or to add a reedy thickening of tone to the clean-sounding diapason chorus of unisons, octaves and fifths. Compound stops of this kind, unlike chorus mixtures, do not break, at least not in the solo range of the compass above about middle C. Fuller descriptions of them are given in Part III.

The three types of chorus just described, together with various subsidiary stops, all have their place in the tonal spectrum of a well-equipped organ. We will now see how they fit into the tonal design of the contemporary British organ.

III. Console of the organ at St Vedast Foster Lane, London, by
N. P. Mander Ltd, 1963. The music desk and other fittings are removed
to show the tracker action. The roller-boards which convey the
mechanical movements laterally can be clearly seen.

IV

The British Organ (1): Tonal Structure

The Importance of Tonal Design

It was said at the end of Chapter II that if an organ is to serve a practical musical purpose, the stops must be disposed in accordance with an intelligent tonal design. Tonal design is the choice and disposition of stops according to the musical function an organ is meant to fulfill. No amount of artistic voicing can make up for the deficiencies of a faulty tonal design.

Organs can be designed either as general or special-purpose instruments. The tonal needs of different periods of musical history differ widely, and nowhere is this more apparent than in the history of the organ. Until the period following the Second World War, nearly all organs were special-purpose instruments, designed to meet the peculiar musical needs of their time. The organs for which Gibbons and Bull, Buxtehude and Bach, Franck and Widor, Parry and Stanford composed their music all differed widely in their tonal schemes. This will be made clear in Part II. Today, special-purpose organs are still made for the performance of certain kinds of music—the German Baroque school, for instance—or for the accompaniment of a certain kind of church service. Nevertheless, a new conception of tonal design has gained acceptance, particularly in Britain: the conception of the general-purpose organ, capable of realizing, within the scope of a limited number of stops, all important schools of organ music from the fourteenth to the twentieth centuries, as well as meeting the needs of choral accompaniment. The modern British organ is looked upon as an eclectic instrument, embracing the essentials of all important organ-building periods, yet retaining a unique national character.

During the following account of the tonal structure of the British organ, it should be borne in mind that many of the organs which the student will encounter fall sadly short of the all-purpose ideal. Some of their shortcomings will be mentioned. Nevertheless, there are many fine organs to be found in Britain today, and the most satisfying of them embody all, or at least some, of the principles of tonal design we are about to consider.

Designation and Order of Manuals

Manuals are numbered from the lowest to the highest: manual I, manual II, and so on. The number of manuals an organ can possess varies from one to five, the latter number being rare and the practical limit. In a two-manual organ the divisions are normally disposed thus:

Manual I   great organ
Manual II swell organ

Occasionally the second division is unenclosed and the disposition is:

Manual I   great organ
Manual II positive organ

In organs of three or four manuals, the order is invariably:

Manual I   choir (and/or positive) organ
Manual II   great organ
Manual III swell organ
Manual IV   solo organ*

---

* In many editions of organ music the great is indicated as manual I, the swell as manual II and the choir as manual III. Unfortunately there is no consistency of practice.

In a five-manual console the highest keyboard may control a bombarde or an echo organ. But the provision of a fifth keyboard is usually more a matter of prestige than artistic necessity. Five manual divisions can quite easily be controlled from a four-manual console, and it is probably better that they should be. Two divisions can be allocated to one manual (for example, both choir and positive organs are playable from manual I at the Royal Festival Hall). Or the fifth division can be 'floating', that is to say, transferable by means of a switch or knob to whichever manual happens to be convenient. This practice avoids the inconvenience of having an upper keyboard which can never be really comfortable to reach, and which also makes it necessary to place the music desk uncomfortably high.

We can now consider in turn the various divisions of the British organ and their individual tonal character. Each may be thought of as consisting of a nucleus of chorus stops together with some subsidiary stops which, although ancillary to the main chorus structure, contribute to the essential character and musical function of the division.

The Great Organ

The great organ is and always has been the main division of the instrument because it contains the major diapason chorus. Its name derives from the early development of the organ, when 'grand' and 'positive' organs were combined under the control of one performer.* The standard contents of a modern great organ, varying according to the overall size of the instrument, are:

The primary diapason chorus, forming the tonal backbone of the whole organ
A group of flutes
In a small two-manual organ, a quiet accompanimental salicional or dulciana

* See p. 82.

A solo cornet V ranks; or a diapason tierce or sesquialtera II
ranks (which can be used with other stops to form a
cornet)

Chorus reeds, varying between a single 8 ft stop and a complete chorus, 16 ft, 8 ft, and 4 ft

The diapason chorus is usually as complete as the size of the
organ will allow. In order of priority of introduction into
minimum schemes the stops are: open diapason 8 ft, principal
4 ft, fifteenth 2 ft, a mixture of at least three ranks, twelfth $2\frac{2}{3}$ ft
or nineteenth $1\frac{1}{3}$ ft, and a double open diapason (or less preferably a bourdon or quintaton) 16 ft. No diapason chorus is
complete without a mixture; indeed, in some small schemes the
mixture is given precedence over the open diapason 8 ft, for
which the cheaper stopped diapason or gedeckt—already
present as part of the flute family—can effectively be substituted.
The mixture is properly kept free of third-sounding ranks.
These, it will be remembered, add a reedy thickness to the
chorus that soon becomes aurally tiring. The stops containing
third-sounding ranks (tierce, sesquialtera, cornet) are separately
available as solo or chorus colouring matter.

The great organ group of flutes provides tonal contrast and
relief to the diapasons, and fills them out in combination.
When possible it is desirable for the family to be completed by
a full-toned 2 ft flute, which is particularly valuable in balanced
trio registration where the diapason 2 ft would be too bright.
The flutes should be capable of blending with the diapasons.
Many ultra-pure clarabellas, Hohlflöten and harmonic flutes
made during the past half-century or so cannot do this. Full-
toned, gently blown stopped diapasons or chimney flutes, found
in most old organs and all well designed modern ones, are best
for this purpose.

The ideal of a musical great organ flue chorus is a combination of dignity, brilliance and polyphonic clarity. This is
achieved by stops of precise attack, well designed mixtures and
balance between the various pitches, no particular pitch—not
even the unison—predominating unduly. Flue choruses of the

seventeenth- eighteenth- and early-nineteenth-century organ builders were generally designed on these principles. During the late nineteenth and early twentieth centuries, however, it was thought that the unison pitch ought to predominate considerably. Consequently, any largish British great organ had as its basis a big concentration of unison tone (often three or more 8 ft diapasons of graduated power) in relation to which the upperwork was meagre and insignificant. (We have seen that the doubling of unisons is an impractical method of chorus-building, and that well designed mixtures contribute to polyphonic clarity). This concentration of the tonal mean of the chorus at unison level and the watering down of the upperwork caused the full chorus to be bottom-heavy and wearisome, but worst of all unclear and lacking in definition.* Polyphonic music (which forms the bulk of the classical organ repertoire) could not be made intelligible upon it.

Many of these pot-bellied great organs still survive in the second-half of the twentieth century; but modern tonal design has reacted against them in the form of better balanced choruses, designed on the principles of the earlier builders.

The solo cornet effect is demanded by much seventeenth- and eighteenth-century music, the layout of which requires it to be on the great organ, where it can be accompanied by or used in duo with the stops of other manuals. It must also be available for use with the great reed chorus where one is provided.†

The basic flue chorus character of the great organ makes the provision of great chorus reeds a secondary consideration. In medium-size schemes the first great reed will usually be an 8 ft trumpet, for solo use and to add a blaze of colour to the full organ. But the provision of a complete great reed chorus is subservient to the prior provision of one on the swell since, as we shall see, the latter is part of the essential character of that department. It is vital that any great reeds there are should not cloud the transparency of the flue chorus. They should colour

---

* Ultra-brilliance can also be wearisome, but this is to go to the opposite extreme.

† For the *grand jeu* of classical French organ music, see p. 100.

not obliterate it. And to do so, they must also be transparent in tone. Great organs of the period when big unison diapasons were fashionable were usually dominated by a set of loud, opaque-toned reeds (usually trombas) that only added to the tonal confusion already existing. Chorus reeds of this kind are no longer made by our leading organ builders.

The specification of the great organ at Wimborne Minster may be quoted as an example of a complete yet economical great tonal scheme, designed in accordance with the principles outlined above:

WIMBORNE MINSTER (1):* GREAT ORGAN
(J. W. Walker & Sons Ltd, 1965)

1. Quintaton	16 ft
2. Open diapason No. 1	8
3. Open diapason No. 2	8
4. Rohr flute	8
5. Dulciana	8
6. Principal	4
7. Koppel flute	4
8. Twelfth	$2\frac{2}{3}$
9. Fifteenth	2
10. Sesquialtera (12–17)	II ranks
11. Mixture (19–22–26–29)	IV ranks
12. Trumpet	8
13. Clarion	4

The Swell Organ

Organ music of the romantic period and accompaniment of the Anglican type of choral service require one organ division to be subject to the expression of a swell box. Since the second quarter of the nineteenth century, therefore, the swell organ has been the customary secondary division in British two-manual schemes.

* See also pp. 50, 53 and 56.

The Swell Organ

A complete modern swell organ will contain:

A reed chorus—except in large schemes the primary reed
chorus of the whole organ
A diapason chorus complete to mixture
A group of flutes and strings
Special non-chorus and solo reeds

As the basic character of the great organ is that of an imperturbable unenclosed flue chorus, so the swell organ has its own
unique chorus character—that of an expressive reed chorus,
which can be used in splendid contrast to the great, or to provide
by means of swell pedal adjustments a background of varying
intensity when both divisions are coupled. In complete form the
reed chorus comprises a family of chorus reeds, 16 ft, 8 ft and
4 ft and a sparkling mixture, the whole matching the great
diapason chorus, or at least great to fifteenth, in volume. This
four stop chorus is the 'full swell'—at its best a spine-tingling
blaze of tone, in which the 16 ft reed and mixture are the chief
ingredients. These two stops, in fact, produce the essence of the
full swell effect by themselves. They are consequently given
priority of introduction over less important stops (such as a
flue double or even the 8 ft and 4 ft chorus reeds) in tonal
schemes of minimum size.

Of equal musical importance to the reed and mixture full
swell, indeed of greater importance in two-manual schemes, is
the swell diapason chorus. Much organ music, particularly of
the seventeenth- and eighteenth-century French and German
schools, requires primary and secondary diapason choruses on
different keyboards. Many of J. S. Bach's organ works, in
particular, demand two bold choruses of equal volume but
contrasted quality. The primary diapason chorus is always on
the great. The secondary one, in the majority of British organs,
is on the swell.

The general failing of the average British swell organ is that
all the power and brilliance of the full swell is derived from the
reeds, the fluework being too weak to function as an adequate
secondary chorus. In well-designed modern organs, however,

49

the swell fluework (with the box open) will be designed to serve as a proper secondary chorus, as loud, or nearly as loud as the great. Contrast with the great is obtained by a higher level of brilliance, derived from narrower scaling and a more acutely pitched mixture. In three-manual schemes the proper place for the secondary diapason chorus is on the unenclosed choir or positive organ. Nevertheless, the swell one should still be strong and telling.

Enclosure makes the swell organ an appropriate home for a few stops which can be subdued by the swell box to provide the warmer and more romantic aspect of the instrument—8 ft and 4 ft flutes, string tone and undulating stops,* and quiet reeds such as the organ type oboe and vox humana. These effects are needed for much organ music of the romantic period as well as for liturgical accompaniment.

The swell tonal design at Wimborne is an excellent example of a good modern swell organ with no unnecessary tonal frills:

WIMBORNE MINSTER (2): SWELL ORGAN
(J. W. Walker & Sons Ltd, 1965)

14.	Open diapason	8 ft
15.	Stopped diapason	8
16.	Viola	8
17.	Vox angelica T. C.†	8
18.	Principal	4
19.	Flute	4
20.	Twelfth	$2\frac{2}{3}$
21.	Fifteenth	2
22.	Mixture (22–26–29)	III ranks
23.	Double trumpet	16
24.	Cornopean	8
25.	Hautbois	8
26.	Clarion	4

* See Part III, *Voix celeste,* for an explanation of this term.
† Tenor C.

Choir and Positive Organs

The function of the lowest keyboard in organs of three manuals or more has changed more during the past century of British organ building than any other division. Today this keyboard will be found to control what is described as a 'choir organ', or a 'positive organ', or both. To explain the character and function of these departments requires more delving into organ history than has hitherto been necessary for the purpose of this book.

The name of the choir organ (as we shall see when we examine the development of the British organ in more detail) is not derived from any function of choral accompaniment. It is a corruption of 'chair organ', the secondary department of the British organ during the seventeenth and eighteenth centuries. The chair or choir organ of this period was generally thought of as a lesser great, bright in tone, but less bold and considerably more restricted in its tonal pallet than its classical German counterpart, the 'positive organ'. The latter contained a full-blooded secondary flue chorus, able to match up to the great in the big preludes and fugues of J. S. Bach, as well as bold and colourful solo mutation and reed effects of a kind which were absent from the British choir organs.

When the swell supplanted the choir as the main secondary department, during the nineteenth century, the choir soon ceased to have a clearly defined musical function. By the end of the century there was a total lack of agreement as to what its tonal character ought to be. In a few schemes, notably in the organs made by Harrison & Harrison during the first half of the twentieth century, it survived as an unenclosed miniature great, too weak to serve as an adequate secondary flue chorus in Bach. But as a general rule it had become a solo-accompani-mental division, sometimes enclosed, and of rather subdued and indeterminate tonal character. During the 1930s a few flute mutations began to appear; but, in keeping with the rest of the division, these were generally too weak to serve effectively

51

as classical solo mutations. Sometimes the great reeds, or a tuba, were made available on the choir manual where they could be solo-ed against the rest of the organ. The specification of the choir organ at the Church of the Sacred Heart, Wimbledon, is a typical example of this kind of tonal conception. All the stops are enclosed with the exception of Nos. 2, 7 and 15.

CHURCH OF THE SACRED HEART, WIMBLEDON:
CHOIR ORGAN
(J. W. Walker & Sons Ltd, 1912 and 1935)

1.	Contra gamba	16 ft
2.	Open diapason	8
3.	Lieblich gedeckt	8
4.	Gamba	8
5.	Dulciana	8
6.	Vox angelica	8
7.	Gemshorn	4
8.	Harmonic flute	4
9.	Nazard	$2\frac{2}{3}$
10.	Piccolo	2
11.	Tierce	$1\frac{3}{5}$
12.	Septieme	$1\frac{1}{7}$
13.	Clarinet	8
14.	Orchestral oboe	8
15.	Tuba	8

Since the Second World War, in many important new and rebuilt instruments, the choir division has been modelled on the principle of the German positive. Because of this, it is sometimes designated 'positive organ' in order to show that it is different from choir organs of the 'solo-accompanimental' or 'miniature great' type. Unfortunately, as so often happens with organ matters, there is no consistency of practice. Many new 'choir' organs are in fact 'positives'. Occasionally the lowest manual will be found to control two departments: an unenclosed positive and an enclosed choir, the latter being a solo-accompanimental section. This is all very confusing, but it is a consequence of the transitional state of British organ building in the late 1960s. One thing is certain: when the reader has become familiar with a true positive, whether it is called 'positive' or 'choir', he will be in no risk of confusing its tonal character with that of a debased choir organ of the late nineteenth and early twentieth centuries.

A modern choir-positive department will contain the following features:

> A bold diapason chorus complete to mixture—usually based on an 8 ft stopped flute—comprising the principal secondary chorus of the instrument
>
> A family of wide-scaled flutes, including solo mutations
>
> An organ-type solo reed, usually a Krummhorn
>
> In a three-manual design (where there is no solo organ), perhaps a powerful trumpet or tuba-type solo reed

The first three items are needed to deal authentically with seventeenth- and eighteenth-century French and German organ music. The solo trumpet or tuba does not form part of the choir-positive organ as such. Its provision on the lowest keyboard is simply a convenience to allow it to sing out a tune against the great and swell organs combined, either as a manual solo or coupled to the pedals.

The positive organ at Wimborne Minster provides an admirable example of a concise tonal design embodying these features:

WIMBORNE MINSTER (3): POSITIVE ORGAN
(J. W. Walker & Sons Ltd, 1965)

27. Gedeckt	8 ft
28. Principal	4
29. Chimney flute	4
30. Quint	$2\frac{2}{3}$
31. Blockflute	2
32. Tierce	$1\frac{3}{5}$

(*continued over page*)

33. Larigot	$1\frac{1}{3}$
34. Sifflute	1
35. Cymbal (29–33–36)	III ranks
36. Krummhorn	8
37. Orchestral trumpet	8

The Pedal Organ

Much of the majesty of an organ is due to the 16 ft tone of the pedal division, which provides the normal bass foundation of the instrument. The unison pitch of the pedals, it will be remembered, is 16 ft, an octave below that of the manuals.

The contents of the pedal organ, like any other division, are, or should be, determined by musical needs. They should be disposed so as to provide:

An independent and clearly defined bass line for the manual flue and reed choruses and lesser effects

Independent solo effects at 8 ft, 4 ft and 2 ft pitches for use against manual accompaniment

In other words, the pedal organ should be a complete and self-contained organ, with its own chorus upperwork and solo stops, just like a manual division (as it was in Germany during the late seventeenth and eighteenth centuries).

By these standards the pedal divisions of many British organs are hopelessly inadequate. The tardy introduction of pedals into the British organ* and the reluctance of conservative organists to understand them led to the mistaken belief that the role of the pedals was merely to *support* the manuals. Thus, pedal divisions of quite large nineteenth-century organs were designed to provide little more than a weighty 16 ft under-pinning to the manuals, and with a few notable exceptions (the early organs of William Hill, for example) contained nothing above 8 ft pitch. The pedal organ at Wimborne Minster, before re-designing in 1965, is a typical example:

* See p. 122.

54

The Pedal Organ

WIMBORNE MINSTER (4): FORMER PEDAL ORGAN

Open diapason (wood)	16 ft
Violone	16
Bourdon	16
Principal	8
Trombone	16

Many pedal organs, no better disposed than this one, will be found today. In many small organs there is nothing more than a solitary bourdon 16 ft.

Such a pedal organ is useless without the help of manual-to-pedal couplers. Its defects are most noticeable in the performance of polyphonic music, for two reasons. Firstly, if the pedals are permanently coupled to the great in loud playing, there will be insufficient tonal contrast between the bass and tenor parts for them to be clearly distinguishable. A weighty pedal 16 ft kills the tenor line; an under-weight one saves the tenor but weakens the bass; and a compromise is hard to attain. For contrapuntal clarity the pedal and manual basses must be balanced but tonally differentiated, and this can only be achieved by independent pedal upperwork. The lack of pedal upperwork can be slightly mitigated by coupling to a spare manual (see page 152), but this is inconvenient and rarely a satisfactory solution. Secondly, there are many passages, particularly in J. S. Bach's music, where the pedal bass meets or moves above the left-hand tenor. An example is the following well-known passage from the Toccata in F:

55

Unless the pedal organ has its own upperwork, the tenor and bass lines is such a passage become merged in confusion.

Chorale preludes by composers of various periods—not only by Bach—often require the tune to be played as a pedal solo on high-pitched stops. Unless the pedal organ has independent upperwork, the required effects can only be obtained by coupling the pedals to a spare manual, thereby immobilizing it for other purposes for the duration of the piece.

Inadequate pedal organs of the kind just described are happily becoming part of bad British history. Most new tonal schemes by leading organ builders contain as fully developed a pedal organ as possible. An example is the re-designed pedal scheme at Wimborne given below. The number of stops allocated to the pedals must obviously depend on the overall size of the instrument. But one with any pretention to completeness will contain a diapason or principal chorus (16 ft, 8 ft, $5\frac{1}{3}$ ft, 4 ft and mixture) and various softer voices including flutes 8 ft, 4 ft and 2 ft. Manual doubles are often duplexed on the pedals for extra variety. A large pedal organ really needs a 32 ft flue stop, open or stopped, and this is seriously missed at Wimborne. Only for very large schemes of cathedral size is the considerable expense of a 32 ft reed justified. The 16 ft chorus reed, however, is a very important stop which should be provided as early as possible in schemes of minimum size. Although it provides a bass to the manual reeds, it should not be too loud for use with the pedal flue chorus as a contrasted bass to the great diapason chorus up to mixture. This effect is comparable to the *organo pleno* (a full organ combination) of J. S. Bach's day. As we shall see when we come to discuss the registration of Bach's music on the modern organ, it is a tonal combination of great importance.

WIMBORNE MINSTER (5): REDESIGNED PEDAL ORGAN
(J. W. Walker & Sons Ltd, 1965)

38.	Principal	16 ft
39.	Violone	16
40.	Bourdon	16

41. Salicional	16
42. Octave	8
43. Bass flute	8 (from No. 40)*
44. Salicet	8 (from No. 41)
45. Octave quint	5⅓ (from No. 40)
46. Fifteenth	4 (from No. 42)
47. Octave flute	4 (from No. 40)
48. Nachthorn	2
49. Mixture (19–22–26–29)	IV ranks
50. Trombone	16
51. Krummhorn	16 (part from No. 36)
52. Posaune	8 (from No. 50)
53. Clarion	4 (from No. 50)
54. Schalmai	2

So far we have considered great, swell, choir or positive and pedal organs, and have illustrated them by reference to the tonal design of an existing three-manual organ. This treatment has been adopted for a special reason. Three manuals and pedals is the ideal size for an organ designed to deal with all schools of organ composition. Much organ music is laid out for a three-manual instrument, and cannot be performed adequately or conveniently with less. The provision of manual divisions in excess of three however, is largely a matter of luxury or convenience. Except in special circumstances it cannot reasonably be held to be essential on strictly musical grounds. We will now consider what these extra or luxury divisions are. They can be explained quite briefly.

The Solo Organ

As its name implies, this division exists primarily for solo purposes. Normally it will be found to contain an assortment of stops of extreme sonority—pure-toned flutes, keen strings, imitative reeds and invariably a tuba. Because of their highly

* Explained on p. 65.

individual character stops of this kind are more suitable for solo than for combinational use, and it is convenient to group them in a separate manual where they can be accompanied by any of the others. Since extreme tone colours are bad blenders, a division of this kind will have no real chorus structure. The solo organ at Westminster Cathedral is a fully equipped example; like most of its kind it is enclosed in a swell box including (in this case exceptionally) the tuba:

WESTMINSTER CATHEDRAL: SOLO ORGAN
(Henry Willis & Sons Ltd, 1926)

Quintaton	16 ft
Tibia	8
Violoncello	8
Cello celeste	8
Salicional	8
Unda maris	8
Concert flute	4
Piccolo harmonique	2
Cor anglais	16
Corno di bassetto	8
Orchestral oboe	8
Orchestral trumpet	8
French horn	8
Tuba magna	8

Solo divisions of this kind are a survival from the early days of the century when orchestral transcriptions were still featured in recital programmes and it was considered necessary for a large organ to contain many orchestral imitations. In the second half of the twentieth century it is generally accepted that the repertoire of the organ is sufficiently varied without the need to resort to orchestral transcriptions, and that any attempt to turn the organ into a one-man band only detracts from its essential dignity.

IV. Three manual and pedal drawstop console, Wimborne Minster, J. W. Walker & Sons Ltd, 1965. Note the angled drawstop jambs and the combination pedals provided instead of toe pistons as in Plate II—a matter of personal preference.

Orchestral imitations, therefore, tend to appear less in modern tonal schemes. There is a feeling that the solo organ should contain only stops of a true organ character, and that it should have an overall chorus structure contributing in some measure to that of the whole organ. Solo mutations rightly find a place in such a division as well as the powerful unenclosed orchestral trumpet or tuba. The result is something like the enclosed solo-accompanimental choir organs of the 1930s, but with less fancy stops and a more dominant flue chorus structure. The enclosed solo organ at St Thomas-the-Martyr (University Church), Newcastle-upon-Tyne is probably the most typical modern example that can be quoted:

ST THOMAS, NEWCASTLE-UPON-TYNE: SOLO ORGAN
(Harrison & Harrison, 1961)

Bourdon	16 ft
Dulciana	8
Spitzflöte	8
Unda maris	8
Nachthorn	4
Octave	4
Open flute	2
Quint	$1\frac{1}{3}$
Sifflöte	1
Sesquialtera	II ranks
Clarinet	8
Orchestral trumpet	8

The Bombarde Organ

This division derives from the eighteenth-century French *clavier des bombardes,* a manual containing one or more loud chorus reeds. The modern bombarde organ consists of a family of powerful, heavy-winded trumpets or tubas, sometimes backed by a powerful diapason chorus with brilliant mixture-work: in

F   59

other words, a much magnified version of the reed and mixture full swell. Powerful registers of this kind do not form part of the normal chorus structure; and it is convenient to have them on a separate manual where they can be used apart from, and in contrast to, the main choruses.

Bombarde divisions are found only in abnormally large instruments where great power is needed to lead and support massed singing. The large organ in the Anglican Cathedral at Liverpool (Willis, 1924) has a bombarde division consisting of tubas 16 ft, 8 ft and 4 ft and a flue grand chorus of 10 ranks. Circumstances where ultra-powerful effects of this kind are musically justified are so rare that they may be disregarded for practical purposes. It is hard to think of an instance where a separate bombarde division is called for in the context of organ music.

The Echo Organ

An echo organ in the modern sense is a division voiced with extreme refinement of tone, sometimes a separate small organ placed at a distance from the main instrument. It should not be confused with the old English echo organ, a short-compass solo division which was the precursor of the swell. The modern echo organ is a fancy division designed purely for ethereal and distance effects, and a luxury very low in the order of organ priorities. It is often found in large organs in the USA, but rarely in Britain.* There is a very beautiful example at Tewkesbury Abbey. It is enclosed, and located in the apse of the Abbey together with solo and separate pedal divisions.

* The echo organs at Westminster Abbey (Hill, 1895) and Norwich Cathedral (Norman & Beard, 1899), both placed at a distance, were not connected up during the last re-builds of these instruments. In the Liverpool Cathedral organ (Willis, 1925) a large echo organ was prepared for but never installed.

Couplers

Couplers

TEWKESBURY ABBEY: ECHO ORGAN
(J. W. Walker & Sons Ltd, 1949)

Quintaton	16 ft
Dolce	8
Unda maris	8
Cor de nuit	8
Dolcissimo	4
Flauto amabile	4
Harmonia aetheria (12–15)	II ranks
Voix humaine	8

Couplers

It will be recalled that the main purpose of couplers is to augment the resources of an organ by enabling two or more division to be used together. Without couplers the tonal resources of an organ would be considerably diminished since the various divisions could only be used separately and no real full organ effect would be possible.

The name of coupler is always self-explanatory. There are three main kinds:

Manual to pedal: enabling manual divisions to be coupled to the pedals. Every organ will have one for each manual. For example, a three-manual organ, such as at Wimborne Minster, will have couplers for 'great to pedal', 'positive (or choir) to pedal' and 'swell to pedal'. A four-manual organ will have in addition a 'solo to pedal' coupler.

Inter-manual: enabling one manual division to be coupled to another. The normal practice is to provide for each manual to be coupled to the great (e.g., by means of a 'swell to great', 'positive (or choir) to great', 'solo to great', etc); and for other manuals to be coupled to each other in an upward direction (e.g., 'swell to choir', 'solo to choir', but not 'choir to swell').

Octave and sub-octave couplers: enabling a particular manual to be coupled an octave higher or lower on itself, e.g., 'swell octave', 'swell sub-octave'. These are seldom provided for the great organ, but often for other divisions. Octave couplers are usually provided in conjunction with a device labelled 'unison off'. The effect of this is to silence the actual notes being played, leaving the octave or the sub-octave brought on by the octave couplers to sound alone, so that the division can be transposed up or down an octave within the limits of the compass.

Manual to pedal and inter-manual couplers, unless otherwise stated on the stop label, work at unison pitch; that is, they actuate the corresponding notes of the division which is being coupled. But some organs are provided with couplers of this kind operating at octave and sub-octave pitches. For instance, 'great octave to pedal' or 'great 4 ft to pedal' couple the great to the pedals an octave above unison pitch. Similarly 'swell octave to great' and 'swell sub-octave to great' couple the swell to the great an octave above or below unison respectively. When these inter-manual and manual to pedal octave couplers are provided in addition to the normal kind, the latter do not 'work through' the unison inter-manual couplers. For example, suppose one is playing on the great organ coupled to the swell by means of the 'swell to great' coupler. It the 'swell octave' is drawn it will be of effect only if one is actually playing on the swell manual. To make the swell sound at octave pitch on the great manual it will be necessary to draw the 'swell octave to great'. It will be seen that many possibilities of registration are opened up by couplers of this kind.

The disadvantage of octave couplers generally is that unless they are used with extreme care they can completely upset the tonal balance of a division, particularly when mixtures are drawn. For this reason the modern tendency is to limit them as much as possible, usually to the swell organ. A well designed tonal scheme is self-sufficient without octave couplers, but if used judiciously they can make an inadequate organ sound much better than it is. More will be said about this when we discuss the registration and use of the organ.

The Extension System

Up to now we have been considering organs built with independent ranks of pipes to each stop. This is known as the traditional or 'straight' system of tonal design. Some organs, however, are constructed wholly or partly on the 'extension', 'transmission' or 'unit' system in which stops of two or more different pitches are derived from a single rank of pipes by means of electric action.

The following illustration will make this clear. Suppose the diagram given below represents a stopped diapason 8 ft of five octaves (or 61 notes, the modern manual compass) each dot representing one pipe:

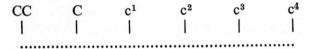

By adding an extra octave of pipes to the treble, making a total of 73 pipes, and by planting them on a sliderless wind chest (see page 16), an appropriate series of pipes can be wired up to the 61 manual keys to form either a stopped diapson 8ft or a flute 4ft as desired:

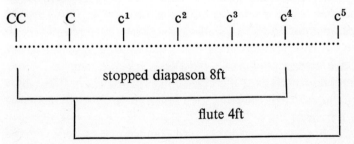

By carrying this process some stages further, a stopped diapason rank of 97 pipes (extending from CCC to c^6) can provide five stops: bourdon 16 ft, stopped diapason 8 ft, flute 4 ft, nazard $2\frac{2}{3}$ ft and piccolo 2 ft.

The extension system can be applied to any class of organ

tone, and the parent ranks are called 'units'. For example, an 85-note trumpet unit (CCC to c^5) may give a double trumpet 16 ft, trumpet 8 ft and clarion 4 ft. An 85-note open diapason unit (CC to c^6) can appear as open diapason 8 ft, principal 4 ft and fifteenth 2 ft, and there are many other possibilities. Even mixtures may be derived from units. The out-of-tuneness of fifth-sounding pitches derived from units tuned to equal temperament is so slight as to be scarcely noticeable; but the true tuning of third-sounding ranks differs so widely from the tempered scale that they cannot satisfactorily be derived from units which are used in unison and octave pitches. If third-sounding pitches are introduced into extension schemes separate ranks must be provided.

The use of a unit is not confined to any particular division, and it can appear in different pitches on different divisions.

The attraction of the extension system is that comparatively few pipes can be made to do the work of many. Judiciously used it can save money and space; but there are one or two snags to which attention should be drawn.

The construction of a chorus from extended units involves a degree of compromise. A rank which is ideally adjusted, say, as an open diapason 8 ft will sound unsatisfactory if it appears as a principal or fifteenth. For a rank to sound satisfactory at two or more pitches, various voicing adjustments, particularly of scaling, must be made, with the result that an extended chorus cannot sound as well as a straight one composed of independently adjusted stops. But it cannot be denied that some effective extension choruses have been made by clever faking.

The biggest snare of the extension organ is that of 'missing' notes. Suppose the following two notes are held on an independent 8 ft stop:

If an independent 4 ft stop is added, the effect will be:

But if a 4 ft stop extended from the 8 ft is added the effect will only three pipes sounding instead of four:

The fact that a note is missing can be detected by repeating the key of the middle note thus:

The repetitions will be of no effect because the c^1 pipe must sustain in its capacity as the 4 ft extension of the pipe C.

Missing notes may not be really noticeable in predominantly homophonic music; but they can cause a disturbing hiatus in polyphonic playing, when odd notes disappear from inner parts for no apparent reason. The player of an extension organ has to be continually on his guard to avoid selecting combinations where missing notes occur.

In the late 1960s there is probably not one leading tonal designer who would think it worth while building a large extension organ. But it is generally agreed that the extension system can be worth while for small organs where space and funds are limited; or for enhancing the tonal resources of a scheme that is predominantly straight. An example of the former can be seen in the specification and tonal analysis of a small extension organ on pages 66–67. Here considerably more tonal is available than would be possible from a straight organ of comparable cost. An example of the latter is frequently found in the pedal organ. As this is usually played in single notes the snare of missing notes rarely arises, and the saving of large and costly pedal pipes makes extension worth while. Reference to the pedal scheme at Wimborne (page 56), for example, will show that the salicional, bourdon, principal and trombone of 16 ft pitch are all unified ranks from which higher pitches are derived. The pedal Krummhorn 16 ft is also a downward extension of the 8 ft one on the positive.

The British Organ (1): *Tonal Structure*

Compass of Manuals, CC to c⁴, 61 notes
Compass of Pedals, CCC to F, 30 notes

GREAT ORGAN

1.	Double Dulciana T.C.	16 ft
2.	Stopped Diapason	8
3.	Dulciana	8
4.	Principal	4
5.	Flute	4
6.	Twelfth	$2\frac{2}{3}$
7.	Fifteenth	2
8.	Piccolo	2
9.	Mixture	2 ranks

POSITIVE ORGAN

10.	Stopped Diapason	8
11.	Spitzflöte	8
12.	Gemshorn	4
13.	Flute	4
14.	Nazard	$2\frac{2}{3}$
15.	Gemshorn	2
16.	Larigot	$1\frac{1}{3}$
17.	Octavin	1

PEDAL ORGAN

18.	Bourdon	16 ft
19.	Bass Flute	8
20.	Dulciana	8
21.	Fifteenth	4
22.	Octave Flute	4
23.	Twentysecond	2

COUPLERS

24. Great to Pedal
25. Positive to Pedal
26. Positive to Great

Analysis

Rank	Ft	Pipes	Great			Positive				Pedal			
			8	4	2	8	4	$2\frac{2}{3}$	$1\frac{1}{3}$	16	8	4	2
Bourdon	16	97	8	4	2	8	4	$2\frac{2}{3}$	$1\frac{1}{3}$	16	8	4	2
Principal	4	61		4	2†		4					4	
Dulciana	8	61 (16 T.C.)	8			8 ø					8		
Spitzflöte	4	61			$2\frac{2}{3}$		4	2†	1†				
*Mixture	$\frac{2}{3}-\frac{1}{2}$ II ranks	74	II ranks			II ranks							
		354											

ø Bass from Bourdon rank   † Top notes from Bourdon rank

*Composition of mixture

CC to BB	26	29
C to g²	19	22
g² sharp to c⁴	12	15

V

The British Organ (2): Means of Control

The Console

The piece of furniture comprising the manuals, pedals and stop controls from which the organ is played is known as the 'console'. The best organ builders have lavished much craftsmanship upon their consoles, making them sumptuous pieces of furniture, with fine joinery, handsome ivory and ebony-covered keys, stop-knobs of turned wood or ivory, and so on.

It is surprising that even in the present-day advanced technological state of organ building there is no standardization of console dimensions though, at the time of writing, attempts are being made to achieve this by the Incorporated Society of Organ Builders. Differences of dimensions and layout will be found according to the age, size, maker and nationality of an instrument, often according to the whim of the current organist at the time of building. These differences are one of the most disturbing yet fascinating aspects of organ-playing. To contend with them successfully requires an aptitude for adaptability not demanded of other instrumental performers.

These differences must be dealt with in describing the general means of control of the contemporary British organ. They appear in the following main forms.

Stop Controls

The two systems of stop control most frequently found are

drawstops (Plates II, III, IV) or some form of stop-key. The latter can be either the more commonly used hinged type (Plate V) or stop tablets (Plate VI). In simple tracker organs, particularly of the older kind, with mechanical stop action the drawstops are usually set in straight jambs (Plate VII). In modern organs the stop jambs are angled for convenience (Plates III and IV); occasionally they are curved as in the large organs by Messrs Harrison & Harrison at Coventry Cathedral (Plate II) and the Royal Festival Hall. Stop-keys are normally arranged over the upper manual, but in large instruments they may also be arranged in sloping jambs at the sides of the key-boards. The present day tendency is to use stop-keys only for smallish organs (because of their comparative cheapness), and drawstops are generally preferred. The ugly horseshoe-shaped stop-key console of the cinema organ type is not a thing any leading British organ builder would nowadays wish to make.

There will also be found, in addition to drawstops and stop-keys, a few abnormal and obsolete systems of stop control. Examples are the Rothwell system in which the stop-keys of a manual division are placed under the appropriate row of keys, and the illuminated stop-controls of the John Compton Organ Company. Systems of this kind are survivals from the gadget-conscious 1920s and 1930s when much importance was attached to slickness of control.

There is no consistency of console layout, apart from the conventional practice of placing the great drawstops on the right and the swell on the left. Couplers are normally grouped with the department they augment (e.g., great to pedal with the pedal stops; swell to great with the great ones). But occasionally, according to individual preference, all the couplers are grouped together: as in the modern Willis console where the speaking stops are controlled by drawstops and the couplers by a row of rocking tablets over the upper manual.

Manuals

Organ manual keys are shorter than modern pianoforte keys,

and small differences will be found in the width of the octave. In most organs made during the last seventy-five years or so the upper manuals slightly overhang the lower, in order to facilitate the 'thumbing' of a melody on the lower manual and to reduce the distance between the highest and the lowest. In the older organs the keyboards do not overhang. Differences of touch have been dealt with in Part I.

Modern practice in consoles of three or more manuals is to tilt the angle of the highest manual towards, and of the lowest away from, the player in order to avoid the need for awkward adjustments of hand position. The manual compass will also vary according to the age of the organ. During the past century or so it has gradually increased from CC to f^3 (54 notes) to CC to g^3 (56 notes), CC to a^3 (58 notes), and ultimately to the modern five octave compass of CC to c^5 (61 notes). The extension from 58 to 61 notes seems to have been brought about more for the convenience of octave couplers than for any other reason. The musical value of the three extreme treble notes of the 61 note compass scarcely seems worth while. They are rarely called for in organ music and can scarcely avoid making a disagreeable sound. Some important French and German romantic music, however, goes up to a^3, and there is a case for making the 58 note compass standard in future.

Pedals

The difficulties of adjustment arising from different types of pedalboard and their placement are probably more disturbing to the beginner-organist than any other factor.

Most British pedalboards are of the modern radiating and concave type shown in Plate II. The object of this design is to facilitate ease of playing by providing that the layout of the pedal keys follows the natural outward and backward swing of the feet. There is general agreement among modern organ builders that the pedalboard should be centred with its middle D directly under the middle D of the manuals, and the 8 ft 6 ins splay of radiation and concavity of the keys is also fairly generally accepted. But here any precise element of standardization ends: the length of the sharps, the thickness of the keys, the distances between them and the depth and weight of touch are factors that differ according to individual practice and preference.

The modern pedal compass has gradually increased to CCC to G, 32 notes, probably more through a desire to round it off to a neat two-and-a-half octaves than for any musical reason. The majority of pedalboards, however, are CCC to F, 30 notes, and many organ builders still make them of this compass. Old pedalboards of 27-note compass CCC to D, sometimes awkwardly centred, are occasionally found.

Although the radiating and concave design was introduced by Willis in the mid-1850s it caught on slowly and examples of the older type of straight and flat, or straight and concave pedal-boards survive in Victorian organs.

The splayed pedalboard has clearly come to stay in Britain, but some organists—including a few leading recitalists—admit that they prefer their pedalboards straight and flat. In this they are supported by the majority of Continental organists with whom the splayed pedalboard has never found much favour. The 'straight' supporters maintain with some logic, that for accuracy of judging distances it is undesirable for the spaces between the keys to vary at different parts of the board. The root of the matter, however, lies in different approaches to pedal technique, a subject which is outside the scope of this book.

Aids to Registration

There are obvious limits to the stop changes that can be made by hand during a brief moment of time. Most consoles made during the present century, therefore, are equipped with thumb pistons and toe pistons or pedals to enable pre-set combinations to be brought on quickly by a single movement during performance.

The British Organ (2): Means of Control

Thumb pistons (also called 'combination pistons') are placed in rows in the key slips below the manuals they affect. There are also 'general pistons', provided in completely equipped organs, which move the stops of the whole instrument. These are usually placed either above the highest manual (Plate II) or in a separate group under the great organ manual (Plate III). Toe pistons or pedals (also called 'composition pedals') are placed immediately above the pedalboard. Normally the right hand group affect the pedal organ and the left hand group duplicate the swell thumb pistons. 'Combination couplers' enable toe and thumb pistons to be coupled together. For instance, a stop control labelled 'great and pedal combinations coupled' enables the great thumb pistons to operate in addition the combinations pre-set on the corresponding pedal toe pistons, and vice versa.

In many old consoles the combinations are pre-set by the organ builder (though they can usually be changed on request). The modern practice is to make them adjustable at the console, either from a switchboard or by means of a 'setter' or 'capture' piston. With the setter system the combination desired to be set on a particular piston is selected by hand; the piston is then pushed while the setter is held in, and the combination becomes fixed on the piston until it is altered by a similar process.

These are some of the many registrational gadgets incorporated in modern consoles by various builders:

Reversible Pistons

These affect a particular stop, the first push bringing it on, the second taking it off, and vice versa. They are usually applied to couplers in frequent use, e.g., great to pedal, swell to great, and occasionally to a 16 ft pedal reed or 32 ft stop.

Doubles Off

A piston cancelling any 16 ft manual and 32 ft pedal stops which may be drawn.

Full Organ or Sforzando

A 'blind' piston bringing on the full organ without moving the stop controls. An illuminated indicator shows whether it is on or off.

Double Touch Cancelling

An extremely useful device often applied to stop-key and occasionally to draw stops. An extra pressure on a selected stop-key (or extra pull on a knob) takes off all the other stops in the division except the one selected. Thus, the full great can be reduced to, say, a solo trumpet by a single action in a fraction of a second. A switch shutting off this device is always provided to avoid accidents by heavy-handed persons.

Double Touch Pistons

These are combination pistons with two pressures of touch. The first pressure gives a manual combination; a harder pressure gives a balancing combination of pedal stops.

General Cancel Piston

Normally placed on the extreme right of the lowest manual key slip (Plates II and III). This puts in all the stops of the organ. It is a 'must' for largish organs, being a great time saver in recitals, besides preventing the risk of mistakes in registration through stops being left out inadvertently.

Not all organs have accessories of this kind. Many nineteenth-century tracker organs have only a few pre-set composition pedals acting directly on the mechanical draw stop action. Without in any way denigrating modern aids to registration, it must be stressed that an organ without such conveniences (either because they were not invented or could not be afforded) is not for that reason an inadequate musical instrument provided it is well equipped tonally. It is up to the player to overcome mechanical limitations by hand registration and by the choice of suitable music.

Swell and Crescendo Pedals

There are two kinds of pedal in use for controlling the swell shutters of enclosed divisions: the old 'trigger' type used in most nineteenth-century organs and the standard modern 'balanced' type (Figure 1, and Plates II, III, V and VI). The former is placed to the right of the pedalboard. The shutters open when the pedal is depressed by the toe, and the pedal returns when it is removed; but the pedal can be fixed in one or more positions by means of notches in a piece of wood. Most organists prefer the centrally placed oblong or shoe-shaped type on which the whole foot can be placed. This is balanced on a central axis and stays in any required position when the foot is removed. Nevertheless, the old trigger swell pedals are not without advantages. The most effective part of a swell box crescendo is in the initial few milimetres of shutter opening. Thus, with the trigger type, *sforzando* and phrasing effects are possible which are less easily managed with the balanced kind. Also when there is a direct mechanical connexion between pedal and shutters the 'feel' of a trigger swell pedal is very positive, and there is a particular excitement to be derived from 'treading' on a good full swell. With swell pedal technique, as with keyboard touch, it is no less desirable for the organist to be physically aware of the mechanical process he is working.

For a swell box crescendo to be fully effective, the process from open to closed must be mechanically smooth and under the direct control of the player. For this reason direct mechanical connexion—either by rods or cables—is the most positive form of shutter control, and leading modern organ builders use it whenever possible. There are more complicated methods of shutter control, but few are entirely satisfactory. In the modern electro-pneumatic system (which must be used when an awkward layout or a detached console makes direct connexion impracticable) the swell pedal makes a series of electrical contacts and the shutters open in several stages or jerks. When there are enough stages (the best swell engines usually have 16) the transition seems smooth and the jerks are unnoticeable. Cheap mechanisms, however, have less than eight stages, the minimum for the crudest working, and the effect is highly inartistic, to say the least. It is desirable for a non-direct action swell pedal to be weighted and balanced so that it has a positive feel.

The modern Willis 'infinite speed and gradation' swell pedal

V. Two manual and pedal stop-key console by J. W. Walker & Sons Ltd. The stop keys are hinged near the upper ends, and are moved downwards (on) and upwards (off) by a flick of the finger. There is a stop crescendo pedal to the right of the swell pedal.

is so different from the normal kind that a brief description
must be given. Unlike the normal kind it is returned by a spring
to a neutral position when the foot is removed. The amount of
pressure forwards is the measure of the speed at which the
shutters open; the amount of pressure backwards is the measure
of the speed at which they close. Since the position of the pedal
is not necessarily related to the position of the shutters, visual
indicators are provided. A feature of the system is that the
shutters can be held tightly closed and unusually gradual or
quick changes of volume are possible. It requires a special
technique, and opinions differ as to its merits.

The general crescendo pedal (Plates V and VI) is operated
like a normal balanced swell pedal, but brings on all the stops
of the organ gradually in chorus order without moving the stop
controls. As with the full organ or *sforzando* pistons, the
position is shown to the organist by means of an indicator. The
general crescendo is particularly useful for the performance of
the organ music of Max Reger (1873–1916) which abounds in
gradually changing dynamics. The late German romantic organs
for which he composed were provided with a similar device
known as the *Rollschweller,* in which the gradual build up was
effected by a horizontal roller turned by the feet.*

Before passing on to the second part of this book dealing with
the practical use of the organ, the reader ought to know something about the more important of the many hundreds of stops
to be found in British and foreign organs. He is recommended
to study the Select Glossary of Organ Stops (Part III, p. 161) at
this stage.

---

* The author only knows one example of a roller-swell in Britain—at
Buckfast Abbey (J. W. Walker & Sons Ltd.).

PART II

USE OF THE ORGAN

VI

Historical Background

Introduction

Our concern here is with only one aspect of organ playing, the art of registration. Registration is the selection of stops according to the music that is being performed. It is part of organ technique and no less important than the art of playing the notes. Like other aspects of musicianship—e.g. tempo, ornamentation, rubato—it involves taste, judgement, and not least, historical knowledge.

The organ repertoire extends over a longer period of time than that of any other musical instrument. Between the Robertsbridge Codex pieces of 1325 and the compositions of composers such as Schoenberg, Messiaen and Hindemith lies a body of music differing widely in style and in the type of organ for which it was conceived. The modern approach to interpretation requires that all this music should be performed with some regard for the intentions of the composers and the sonorities available to them. Anyone who wishes to make his performances scholarly as well as musical (and one attribute is of little use without the other) will need to keep this continually in mind. His approach to interpretation will need to be objective. If it is not, he will find little of interest in this book, and might just as well play organ music on the pedal pianoforte or, for that matter, the concertina.

The first requisite of an objective approach to registration is a background knowledge of important past organ-building

79

schools and the registrational practice of principal composers. Only when this is understood can their music be realized intelligently on the organs available today.

What are the important past schools of organ-building? The answer depends on how one evaluates the schools of composition that the organs inspired. It would be a very perverse critic, however, who would not agree that one could say—without denigrating other national schools—that the bulk of worthwhile organ music was written for the Italian organ of *c*. 1500 to *c*. 1700, and for the French and German organs of *c*. 1600 to *c*. 1750 and the more eminent of their nineteenth-century successors. This, broadly, is the contemporary view reflected in present-day recital programmes.

Typical instruments of these periods and their use, therefore, must be described; but they cannot meaningfully be isolated from the mainstream of organ tonal history. The background must be sketched in, and the whole presented as a complete, though necessarily brief, survey of the organ's tonal development. Our own early British school must also receive due mention because, though opinions differ as to its importance, there is a revived interest in its music and it forms an essential background to the understanding and use of the modern British organ.

The Gothic Organ

Periods of organ construction have as convenient labels the names of corresponding periods of art history, Gothic, Renaissance, Baroque and so on. These periods are not precise, of course, but overlap and merge imperceptibly into each other.

Though the organ was invented by the third century B.C. at the latest, and by the beginning of the Christian era had been developed by the Romans into a highly sophisticated small organ with balanced keyboard and stops,* we need look no further back than the Gothic era, extending at its widest from

* Called a 'hydraulis' because the wind supply was stabilized by a water container.

about 1250 to 1540. By the beginning of this period the organ—having through the interest of the Arabs, survived the disintegration of the Roman Empire—had been re-invented in Europe and become established as the main musical instrument of the church.

By the mid-thirteenth century the spring-pallet and balanced keyboard had been re-discovered (the earlier medieval organs were played by springless sliders moved in and out by hand) and three distinct types of organ were in use:

Large 'grand' organs, permanently sited on screens or in galleries

Small 'portative' organs which, slung round the neck, were played with one hand and blown with the other

Small 'positive' organs, not transportable in use, that stood either on the floor or on a table

The smaller organs had one or two ranks of pipes to each note; the larger had several ranks, but as yet no stops and consequently no means of varying the volume or tone. The grand organs, in fact, were immense diapason mixtures comprising a chorus of unisons and fifths, for which the German name was 'Blokwerk'. This method of chorus building, as we have seen, was found at an early date to be the only practicable way of constructing a brilliant and ringing chorus. The Blokwerk was the ancestor of the modern diapason chorus since, when a stop mechanism was invented, the lower pitches were gradually detached from it, the higher pitches remaining together as a separate many-ranked compound stop.

Grand organ actions were crude and heavy. The necessarily large keys were put down by the hand or the clenched fist: hence the name *pulsator organorum* given to performers on large Gothic organs. Little dexterity was possible on these instruments. Positive and portative organs, however, were more manageable. That considerable keyboard dexterity was possible by the mid-fourteenth century is attested both by the Robertsbridge pieces and the fame of Francesco Landini's performance on the organetto or portative organ.

81

Players of early grand organs must have quickly felt the need for a 'third hand' to manage the heavy bass action and sustain low drones or pedal points. Such a need was clearly felt in the case of the positive; the well-known van Eyck altar panel at Ghent (1425) shows a positive organ with a latch for sustaining a bass drone. Thus, it is easy to see one reason for the origin of pedals: a few bass pipes were made playable on a pedalboard for musical and physical ease.

Separate keyboard divisions were also well advanced by the mid-fourteenth century. Michael Praetorius in his *Syntagma Musicum* (1619) illustrates the three manual and pedal keyboards of the Halberstad Cathedral organ built by Faber in 1361.* These divisions originated in two different but related ways.

First, it was originally necessary for each pipe to stand more or less above its key: the roller-board, a device for transmitting the key-action laterally, had not been invented. To place all the pipes in a row would have made the keyboard impossibly wide, so pipes and keys had to be arranged in tiers. The pipes of the 'tenor' manual and the basses ('trompes') were arranged in the main case in front of the organist. Those of the treble (the 'descant' manual) were placed in a smaller case behind the player, there being little difficulty in passing the action under his feet.

The second mode of origin is of more significance in the light of later developments. A positive organ might be placed in the gallery alongside a grand organ so that the organist could turn to it for tonal variety and physical relief. From this it was a short step to combine the two organs with their keyboards in tiers. Both organs might be placed in the main case; or the grand (great) organ in the main case and the positive, like the descant division, in a smaller case behind the player's back.

An important result of this splitting up of the organ was a divisional difference of pitch. The great became an 8 ft organ;

* Michael Praetorius (1571–1621); one of the most versatile and prolific musicians of his day. *'De Organographia'*, vol. ii of his *Syntagma Musicum* (fascimile ed. Kassel, 1929) gives an invaluable account of contemporary organs and a glimpse into those of the Gothic period.

the positive in its smaller case became a 4 ft organ, sounding an octave higher; the pedals controlling the longer pipes were a 16 ft organ sounding an octave lower. In this way originated the 'work' or 'division' principle (German: Werkprinzip) of organ disposition which, as we shall see, became an important visual and tonal feature of the organs of the German and French Baroque.

From an early stage the exterior of the organ—the organ case—was made an object of decorative beauty. Case designers were quick to make the most of the pleasing effect of combined great and positive cases, the smaller offsetting and echoing the larger in sight as well as in sound (Plate VIII). The invention of the roller-board soon enabled the compass to be extended, so that the pipes no longer had to stand over their keys and the keyboards could be narrower than the sound-boards. This, too, was reflected in the outward appearance. The main soundboard was gracefully corbelled out from the console, causing the elegant effect of over-hanging sides which has been a particularly delightful feature of well proportioned organ cases ever since.

The Renaissance Organ

The Renaissance era was a transitional period when the intractable Blokwerk organ gradually evolved into the versatile many-voiced organ of the Baroque. It is generally understood as covering the period roughly from 1540 to 1600; but it began sooner in Germany, where maturity came quickly and organ design moved swiftly from Gothic to Baroque with the minimum intervening period.

The Gothic organ could play soft or loud, but had little tonal variety. It was necessary, therefore, for a stop mechanism to be re-invented so that the lower pitches could be detached from the Blokwerk and used separately. This had certainly begun by 1350. The stopping-off of ranks was at first effected, not by sliders, but by the Springlade (spring-chest) in which the wind was cut off from the entire chest on which a particular rank or group of ranks stood. Slider chests were not common until well into the seventeenth century.

In Italy the Gothic organs were split up into separate stops from the start. But in Germany, and no doubt in northern Europe generally, it was only gradually that separate stops were detached from the Blokwerk. Thus a great organ might survive as a Blokwerk with independent stops on the positive only—as at St Bavo, Haarlem, as late as 1630. Or the great might consist of 8 ft, 4 ft and 2 ft principals, the rest of the Blokwerk remaining as a mixture of perhaps as many as fifteen ranks—as at Klosterneuberg Abbey in Austria, where the existing organ dates substantially from 1542.

With the invention of stops came the incentive to develop individual tone colours. Stopped and open flue pipes were known to the pre-Gothic builders; but during the Renaissance period many new flue tone colours were evolved, following the invention of tapered and half-stopped pipe bodies and a variety of scales. The regals, an early type of portative reed organ, were also incorporated into tonal schemes, leading to the development of new types of reed tone. Praetorius lists as many as 25 reed and 74 flue stops of different pitch and tonal quality. This tonal transformation opened up possibilities of stop-selection and encouraged the development of a specific organ repertoire. The outstanding composer-organists of this period were Heinrich Isaac (1450–1547), Jacob Obrecht (1450–1505) and Adrian Willaert (*c.* 1480/90–1542), whose music did much to stimulate a more eloquent use of the instrument.

Thereafter national and regional schools inevitably emerged, and after 1500 they can easily be traced. The German school will be considered first, not only because it was the first to reach maturity, but also because it inspired the bulk of important organ music, culminating with J. S. Bach.

The German Baroque School and the Organ of Bach

For practical purposes the north German school is grouped

with the Dutch: South Germany and Austria developed somewhat differently. Of the two schools the northern assumes
greater importance because it was there that the use of the
pedals was first fully exploited.

The transitional Renaissance organ, as we have seen, had a
Blokwerk great, perhaps partly split up, and a positive containing stops of varying sonorities. From this stage it was a short
step to enable to combine these groups on one manual; then
to apply the composite scheme to other divisions so that each,
pedals included, became completely self-contained with three
tonal families:

A narrow-scale principal chorus completed by the remains of
the Blokwerk
Flue stops of varied construction, mostly wide-scale flutes
A group of reeds

This happened early in the fifteenth century. About the same
time emerged the names of the divisions or works which
strictly followed their placement within the organ. The Hauptwerk (great) was placed in the main case above the player.
Behind him in a separate case was the Rückpositiv (back-
positive). Other manual divisions, Brustwerk (breast-work) and
Oberwerk (over-work) were placed in the main case below and
above the Hauptwerk respectively. The Pedal was placed either
in the outer towers of the main organ case, or divided in two
detached towers on each side of it (Plate IX).

A two-manual organ contained a Hauptwerk and either a
Rückpositiv or a Brustwerk; a three-manual one had a Haupt-
werk, a Rückpositiv and either a Brustwerk or an Oberwerk.
Only rarely were all four manual divisions present in one
instrument, as in the big Schnitger organs at St Michael,
Zwolle or St Jacob, Hamburg.

Placing the Brustwerk immediately above the console within
reach of the player was doubly convenient. First, because it
contained reeds of the regal class which, being notoriously
unstable in pitch, needed to be easily reached for tuning.
Second, the Brustwerk was often provided with doors which the

85

organist could close, changing it at will from a bold positive into an echo division (Bovenwerk).

The work principle was sound both musically and mechanically.

It was musically sound because each division could speak out without obstruction; and because an important spacial dimension was added to the tonal contrast between the divisions. Tonal contrast came initially from the different pitch emphasis of each principal chorus—a feature inherited from the Gothic organ. The pitch emphasis of a division was determined by the length of its longest principal. In a large organ the pedal might be 32 ft, the Hauptwerk 16 ft, the Rückpositiv 8 ft and the Oberwerk or Brustwerk 4 ft, the 8 ft pitch of the latter being borrowed from the flute group. On smaller organs the divisional pitches were an octave higher: Pedal 16 ft, Hauptwerk 8 ft and Rückpositiv 4 ft. Thus, the Hauptwerk was comparatively broad and dignified, the other manuals sharper and more penetrating but little (if at all) softer. This tonal contrast, however, was intensified three-dimensionally by the placement of the divisions. It was particularly noticeable between Hauptwerk and Rückpositiv. The former in its main central position was necessarily more pervasive and diffuse; but the latter, being nearer the listener, was more concentrated and directional. Contrast of this kind is particularly effective in the antiphonal use of manual choruses in Bach's Dorian Toccata (BWV 562) among other works, and it gives a meaning to the music which would not otherwise be apparent.

The work-principle was mechanically sound because it enabled tracker action, the overwhelming advantages of which have been explained earlier, to be applied successfully. The vertical disposition enabled the mechanism to be properly balanced and to take full advantage of the force of gravity so that, even in large organs such as St Michael, Zwolle and St Bavo, Haarlem, the touch was light, crisp and responsive.

The organs of the northern school and the music—the great line of composers from Sweelinck to Bach—grew up hand in hand. As the music culminated with Bach, so organ building

The German Baroque School and the Organ of Bach

reached a peak in the instruments of Arp Schnitger (1648–1719), which are generally regarded as the summit of Baroque achievement and ideal for Bach.

The music of the north German school requires at least two manuals and pedals and a tonal scheme of about thirty speaking stops. Because the larger specifications contain a great deal of tonal duplication, the tonal design and character of the north German Baroque organ is more conveniently illustrated by a specification of this optimum size. An example is the 1659 Schnitger organ at Cappel, the sound of which is well known through the Bach recordings of Helmut Walcha. The stops are classified into the three groups: principals, flutes and reeds.

CAPPEL: ORGAN BY ARP SCHNITGER, 1659

	Principals (narrow scale) 'male'		*Flutes* (wide scale) 'female'		*Reeds*	
HAUPTWERK	Principal	8	Hohlfloit	8	Trompet	8
	Octava	4	Spitzfloit	4		
	Rauschpfeife	II	Nasat	$2\frac{2}{3}$		
	Mixtur	V–VI	Gemshorn	2		
			Quintade	16		
			Zimbel	III		
RUCKPOSITIV	Principal	4	Gedact	8	Dulcian	16
	Octava	2	Floit	4		
	Scharf	IV–VI	Siffloit	$1\frac{1}{3}$		
			Quintade	8		
			Sesquialtera	II		
PEDAAL	Untersatz	16	Nachthorn	2	Posaune	16
	Octava	8			Trompet	8
	Octava	4			Cornet	2
	Rauschpfeife	II				
	Mixtur	IV–VI				

Tremulant; Cymbelstern; Rückpositiv to Hauptwerk.

The Pedaal flue work is given over mainly to a principal chorus 16 ft to mixture, the flute group being represented by the solitary Nachthorn 2 ft which, in practice, would have been combined with the lower pitched principals for solo purposes. The pitch differentiation of the divisions will be apparent: Pedaal 16 ft, Hauptwerk 8 ft and Rückpositiv 4 ft. The two Quintade stops, strictly proper to the flute group, were regarded as belonging partly to the principals because they provided the 16 ft and 8 ft pitches in the Hauptwerk and Rückpositiv principal choruses respectively. The Zimbel and Sesquialtera, though of principal scale, were also regarded as being common to both groups for reasons which we shall see shortly.

Schnitger's organs and the north German school generally differed from the modern British organ* in three important respects:

(1) *Balance*

All the stops were of moderate and more or less equal volume. This ensured a tonal balance between an equal number of stops in each division, an important feature for the playing of trios and works such as the Dorian Toccata, which demands balanced antiphonal choruses. In many modern organs the wide differences of volume between stops and choruses makes satisfactory balanced effects very difficult to achieve.

(2) *Attack*

All the flue stops were voiced on low wind-pressure (about three inches) with a minimum of nicking. They consequently spoke with a quick, precise initiation characteristic—a sort of 'chiff' at the beginning of the note, like the 'lipping' attack of an orchestral flute or the pluck of a harpsichord. This gave the tone much vitality and interest and helped to define the movement of polyphonic parts. The chiffing was more pronounced in the flutes than in the principals. In some modern organs built in Baroque style (neo-Baroque or

---

* The average organ built between roughly 1870 and 1950, such as the reader is most likely to be acquainted with.

The German Baroque School and the Organ of Bach

classical revival) the principals chiff in an exaggerated manner that has no early precedent. Much modern flue-work has been robbed of its vitality and attack by 'romantic' voicing methods involving high wind-pressures and excessive nicking, which is one reason why it is so unsatisfactory for the performance of Baroque music.

(3) *Clarity*

The principal choruses were tonally transparent and the trebles had just the right amount of melodic prominence so that a polyphonic texture could be clearly heard. This was due to several factors: the careful adjustment of the individual ranks, properly arranged mixture breaks and, not least, incisive attack. Chorus clarity is by no means easy to achieve but the Baroque organ builders plainly took much trouble to achieve it. Obviously it was essential that they should, since much Baroque organ music sounds meaningless on instruments which muddle the counterpoint. In most twentieth-century British organs clarity is not a 'built-in' virtue. It can only be attained—if at all—by extreme care in registration.

We will now consider the tonal character of the Schnitger type of organ in a little more detail. In so doing it is necessary to remember that tonal qualities can only be described very inadequately and subjectively in words.

The Principal Chorus

The principal chorus of each division varied, as we have seen, according to its pitch emphasis and space placement. Each foundation principal was of fairly bright singing tone, rather like the few British seventeenth- or eighteenth-century diapasons that have survived unaltered. Each chorus was carried upwards in ranks of more or less equal volume and consisted only of unisons and fifths. The resulting 'clean-sounding' effect was considered to possess an essentially 'male' character. The third-sounding ranks and the wide-scale stops of the flute group were thought of as 'female'. Up to 2 ft pitch the Hauptwerk chorus

89

was comparatively gentle. When the mixtures were added the whole would blaze into life; but even then the chorus was not loud by modern standards—its bright, transparent sound, full yet gentle, could be endured for long periods without aural fatigue. The forward-placed Rückpositiv with its octave-higher foundation was more direct and penetrating. Only when all the manuals were coupled was there anything like a *fortissimo* in the modern sense. Schnitger's mixtures produced a particularly characteristic sound, an intense, 'needly' glitter, full of life and movement. This sound may be heard at its most characteristic in the Schnitger school organ at St Laurens, Alkmaar,* a famous instrument familiar to British listeners, like that at Cappel, through the medium of records and broadcasts.

The Flute Group

The flutes varied greatly in pipe construction and tone quality. They were generally more colourful and better blending than the usual 'pure-toned' modern organ flutes—never muddy or oily—and the initial 'chiff' contributed greatly to their distinctive character. The Gedeckt was fuller and more liquid in tone than the narrow-scale British stopped diapason of the same period or the modern Lieblich Gedeckt. The tapered Spitzflöte and Gemshorn had an elusive flute-string quality due to the emphasis of the fifth upper partial (the seventeenth) and higher harmonics. The chimneyed construction of the Rohrflöte gave it more piquancy and interest than the fully closed Gedeckt. The Quintade family were stops of Gedeckt type, but narrower and with the third harmonic (the twelfth) developed to equal prominence with the ground tone. The partly-tapered Koppelflöte was regarded as a neutral medium for coupling with other tones or as a basis for erecting 'tonal pyramids' of higher-pitched stops.

Also included in the flute group were the solo mutations, designed primarily for synthetic solo tone-building. The wide-scale Nasat 2⅔ ft gave a distinctive nasal quality to any neutral

* Rebuilt in 1723–25 by Frans Caspar Schnitger, one of Arp Schnitger's sons.

VI. Two manual and pedal console with stop-tablet control by Hill, Norman & Beard Ltd. A stop-tablet is centrally balanced. A touch on the bottom end moves it downwards (on); a touch at the top returns it to the upper (off) position. There is a stop crescendo pedal to the right of the swell pedal.

combination. In Germany, unlike France, the tierce was narrow-scaled and never drew separately: it was always joined with a principal scale twelfth in the two-rank Sesquialtera. The latter had a dual role: as a solo mutation (for compounding a cornet or some other reedy sonority) or as a thickening ingredient for the principal chorus, whenever this seemed musically desirable. It was therefore regarded as belonging to both narrow and wide groups impartially. Likewise the Zimbel. This was a very high-pitched compound stop which broke so that the same notes repeated throughout each octave of the compass. It was used either to provide a bell-like overlay in running flute passages, or to add an extra glitter to the full principal chorus.

The Reeds

There were three main classes of reed tone: trumpets, with inverted conical tubes; the Krummhorns, with cylindrical half-length tubes; and regals, with short resonators of varied shapes. All were voiced on the flue-work light wind pressure of about three inches.

The trumpets had open shallots and un-weighted tongues. Those on the manuals were of moderate power, prompt speech and fairly brilliant tone, such as can still be found in some old British organs. They added richness to the principal chorus but little sense of climax. On the whole the manual chorus reeds were inferior to the flue-work, but the pedal ones were better. These were of restrained volume, but of fairly solid tone, which gave a superb definition to the full pedal when used as bass to the principal chorus—in the *organo pleno* effect—without giving the bass too much prominence.

The Krummhorns were akin to the modern organ clarinet, but louder and thinner and without its sugary orchestral quality.

The regals were a group of highly individual 'snarling' sonorities; hence their onomatopoeic name of 'Schnarrwerk'. There were many types, all with short variously-shaped resonators, such as the Trichter, Apfel, and Knop regals with funnel, apple and head-shaped resonators respectively. The vox humana (whose throaty tone quality was supposed to imitate

H 91

the human voice) is a member of the regal class that has persisted into the romantic organ. Because the regal resonators were not proportionate to the pitch of the reed, they were very unstable in tuning. For this reason and because of their somewhat uncultured tone they fell into disfavour during the eighteenth century. Freshly tuned, however, their naïve, bucolic tone can sound peculiarly attractive to modern ears, and highly effective in the right musical context. Regals were normally used with flue stops or mutation effects—seldom alone. Werckmeister* wrote with truth in 1698 that: 'Schnarrwerk is the work of fools, but when it is pure and good it rejoices heart and mind'.

Contemporary Registration

How were the north German Baroque organs used? The answer is drawn from several complementary sources: from hints in theoretical treatises; from the somewhat sparse indications of composers; but mainly from the nature of the instruments and the style of the music. Consideration of the kind of music composed for the north German Baroque organ provides the most convenient mode of explanation. This falls broadly into three main classes.

The first class contains polyphonic music in which no part calls for particular emphasis: for example, the toccatas, preludes and fugues of J. S. Bach and several of his chorale preludes. Such music was intended to be played on all or part of the various principal choruses. Bach writes at the beginning of several pieces, *pro organo pleno* (for full organ).† This was

---

* Andreas Werckmeister (1645–1706): *Orgelprobe* (1698) (fascimile ed. Kassel, 1932), a short work on the 'proving' or testing of organs.

† Among others: Prelude and Fugue in E flat (BWV 552); Prelude in B minor (BWV 544); the chorale prelude *Wir glauben all' an einen Gott, Schöpfer* (BWV 680), sometimes called 'The Giant's Fugue'. Many other works, however, cry out for similar treatment. The term can be traced to the *organo pieno* of sixteenth- and seventeenth-century Italian organs. 'Organo Pleno required full work on the manuals without reeds; but reeds should be added to the pedals.' (J. Mattheson, *Der vollkommene Kapellmeister*, (1739).

undoubtedly the equivalent of the French *plein jeu* (see page 97 below). It did not consist of all the stops in the organ, but normally only of the Hauptwerk and Pedal principal choruses with one or more pedal reeds. Contrasting manual episodes required by the musical structure were played on the flue-work of the Rückpositiv or another secondary division. For a piece requiring very full treatment, two or more principal choruses were coupled in the *pleno*.

In the second class is music in the form of a duo or trio in which each voice calls for an independent and distinct sonority. J. S. Bach's trio sonatas are probably the most obvious examples. The beauty of the Baroque organ for this kind of music was, as explained above, that an equal number of stops on different divisions could be relied upon to balance. Thus, the manual parts of a trio sonata might be represented by flutes 8 ft and 4 ft, or 8 ft, 4 ft and 2 ft on each keyboard, or any of these combinations and a mutation. The pedal part might be represented by flue stops 16 ft, 8 ft and 4 ft, the 16 ft pitch being required by the continuo-style bass. A slow movement might be registered as a manual duo between an 8 ft flute and a Krummhorn or regal, with pedal flues 16 ft and 8 ft.

The third class includes music—mostly chorale preludes—in which one part is meant to be soloed on a distinctive tone colour. The chorale might be given to a 4 ft pedal reed accompanied by manual flutes, as in Bach's *Kommst du nun, Jesu* (BWV 650). Or it might be in coloratura form as in the well-known *Nun komm' der Heiden Heiland* (BWV 659). In the last mentioned kind of piece the colourful solo reeds and synthetic tone colours were especially appropriate. The latter, particularly if used with a slow-beating tremulant, had a haunting beauty well-suited to the contemplative character of the music. The Hauptwerk principal was soft enough to accompany a *mezzo-forte* solo on the Rückpositiv. Again, the spacial dimension of the work-principle system contributed to the musical effect, the solo voice on the forward-placed Rückpositiv being projected against the more expansive backcloth of the Hauptwerk.

Seventeenth-century German registration was governed by

a number of conventions. One forbade the mixing of wide- and narrow-scale groups; another the use of more than one 8 ft stop at a time in chorus. No doubt these, like all rules, were broken from time to time either deliberately or through ignorance. But after about 1700 there is evidence of more freedom in the choice of stops. Adlung* tells us that the rules were often broken by the end of the seventeenth century. And on the authority of Forkel,† Bach himself was an innovator in using new combinations that set aside the old rules.

Dynamics

To what extent was the registration altered in Bach's day during performance? This fascinating and highly controversial question will never be answered conclusively, but an attempt must be made to deal with it here.

Clearly little could be done by the organist himself. The stop action was cumbersome and noisy. A few ventil chests (enabling blocks of stops to be added and withdrawn by means of a pedal) appeared in Bach's lifetime, but there were no other mechanical aids to registration. In many consoles the stop handles could not be reached without getting up from the seat, and the couplers were worked by pulling an entire keyboard out a short distance by means of knobs at the ends.

Stop alterations at other than clearly defined musical breaks, therefore, could only have been made with the help of assistants. Was this done very much? That an assistant was occasionally employed is shown by the score of the Bach-Vivaldi concerto transcriptions in D minor (BWV 596) and A minor (BWV 593) where there are indications that someone was expected to add a 32 ft pedal stop and a coupler. Yet stop changes of this kind can hardly have been considered essential. If they were, it

* Jakob Adlung (1699–1762): organist and teacher; author of *Musica mechanica organoedi* (1768), an important theoretical treatise on the manufacture and care of keyboard instruments.

† J. N. Forkel, *On Johann Sebastian Bach's Life, Genius and Works* (1802); reproduced in David and Mendel, *The Bach Reader*, New York (1945); see p. 314.

would be reasonable to expect the survival of more than a few scores marked with assistant's instructions, but these are conspicuously rare. Again, pre-arranged stop changes would hardly be practicable in improvised performances, and no doubt Bach, at any rate, was more likely to improvise a new piece during or after a church service than to play a composed one. And we have on record Forkel's account of Bach's improvised performances on the organ.*

More important is the question whether the addition or subtraction of stops, as the only means of obtaining a crescendo or diminuendo, is called for by the style of Baroque organ music generally. The answer seems to be almost certainly 'no', because organ and harpsichord composers, at least, did not think in terms of this kind of expression. Their music, in accordance with the nature of the instruments, was conceived in terms of what have been called 'terrace' or, less happily, 'block' dynamics—contrasted terraces or levels of sound, even entire movements, each at the same dynamic intensity. Any climaxes were inherent in the musical structure and called for no extra dynamic emphasis. This is a mode of expression to which organs and harpsichord are uniquely suited. This is not to say that the terraces were flat and monotonous. String and wood-wind players, for instance, naturally apply a slight crescendo to rising passages, and vice versa. Expression of this kind was 'built into' the voicing of the organs; a gradual increase of volume and fullness throughout the ascending compass ensuring that rising and falling passages had just the right amount of dynamic emphasis.

Some musicologists have held that terrace dynamics apply strictly to all Baroque music. This theory, no doubt a natural reaction from the excesses of romantic treatment of old music, no longer holds water. In the light of the evidence one wonders that it was ever thought tenable.† Nevertheless, it is generally accepted that terrace dynamics are to some extent inherent in

* Ibid., pp. 315–16.
† See Robert Donington, *The Interpretation of Early Music* (1963), 2nd. ed., London, 1965, p. 416, where the evidence is set out very clearly.

much Baroque instrumental music: the Italian concerto form, for example. And they cannot help but apply to music written specifically for the organ and the harpischord, since these instruments by their very nature cannot emulate the subtleties of other instruments. Paradoxically, this lack of 'expressiveness' in the Baroque organ becomes its greatest virtue, its impression of imperturbable strength, which the greatest composers have exploited magnificently. When Bach wrote *pro organo pleno* at the beginning of a piece, he meant it to be played throughout on the full principal choruses with all their statuesque dignity. Nothing could be further from this than the romantic practice— happily dying out in the second-half of the twentieth century— of starting such a piece on soft 8 ft stops and gradually working up to a tremendous climax, regardless of the musical architecture.

Rococo and Classical

By the second-quarter of the eighteenth century German organ building began to split up into schools which have been conveniently described as 'rococo' and 'classical'.* The rococo tended towards more dramatic effects, greater divisional contrasts and powerful climax mixtures. Probably its greatest exponent was the Dutch Christiaan Muller whose *magnum opus* is the famous organ at St Bavo, Haarlem, finished in 1738. Because the principal exponent of the classical school was the renowned Gottfried Silberman (1683–1753), who built many organs in central and southern Germany, it became better known and until recently tended to eclipse all others, including that of Schnitger. Silberman's organs were altogether smoother, and more powerful and unified than Schnitger's. Silberman abandoned the careful wide and narrow stop groupings, using varieties of scales, introducing undulating stops and attempts at string tone. Often the vertical work-disposition was over-

* Here the term 'classical' is used in a very special sense, as a convenient tag for a particular manifestation of the classical organ (in the sense explained in the footnote to page 24).

looked and the whole instrument packed into a single case. His pedal organs rarely had the versatility of Schnitger's. Bizarre reed effects such as regals were eschewed and replaced by reed-imitative cornets and mutations. Fine as Silberman's organs were, they contained tendencies that ultimately destroyed the European baroque-rococo-classical organ. By about 1800 the days of this kind of organ building were temporarily over, and musical interest moved increasingly towards romanticism and the development of new means of musical expression such as the modern orchestra and the metal-frame pianoforte with which the static tone of the organ could not compete.

The French School

The French organ of the seventeenth and eighteenth centuries is much less complicated than the German and may be styled 'baroque' or 'classical' according to taste. During this period, as we have seen, the German school varied considerably. But the French school, having reached full maturity by 1575 at the latest, continued with little change until the Revolution, and staggered on into the nineteenth century until it was finally eclipsed by the 'symphonic' organ of Cavaillé-Coll (dealt with in the next section).

Any of several specifications of the period could be quoted as typical. Here, for example, is the stop list of the organ at St Spire, Corbeil, Ile de France, built by G. Joly in 1675, containing three manuals, pedals and twenty-eight speaking stops.

The French school and the north German school had a few features in common. The stops were grouped in similar tonal families, except that the bourdons were used in the *plein jeu* with the principals. Grand and positif divisions were disposed on work principle lines like the Hauptwerk and Rückpositiv and had similar 8 ft and 4 ft pitch foundations. Like the German principal choruses the *plein jeu* consisted purely of unisons and quints. The grand orgue chorus was called 'le grand plein jeu'; that of the positif 'le petit plein jeu'.

97

Historical Background

	Plein Jeu		Jeu de Mutations		Anches (reeds)	
GRAND ORGUE 16 Stops	Bourdon	16	Flûte	4	Trompette	8
	Montre	8	Nasard	$2\frac{2}{3}$	Clairon	4
	Bourdon	8	Quartre de		Voix humaine	8
	Prestant	4	Nasard	2		
	Doublette	2	Tierce	$1\frac{3}{5}$		
	Fourniture	IV	Flageolet	1		
	Cymbale	III	Cornet	V		
POSITIF 8 Stops	Bourdon	8	Nasard	$2\frac{2}{3}$	Cromorne	8
	Montre	4	Larigot	$1\frac{1}{3}$		
	Doublette	2				
	Fourniture	III				
	Cymbale	II				
	Cymbale	II				
ECHO 2 Stops Short Compass			Cornet	V	Voix humaine	8
PEDALE 2 Stops 29 Notes	Flûte	8			Trompette	8

The differences, however, were considerable. Unlike the German pedal divisions, the French pedale was a small 8 ft based solo division, used in trios or for a trompette cantus firmus against the *plein jeu*. Only late in the eighteenth century were 16 ft stops introduced and then rarely—first a bombarde and subsequently a flute, and very exceptionally a 4 ft flute and mutations. The tierce $1\frac{3}{5}$ ft always appeared as a wide-scale flute and separately, which never occurred in Germany.

Contrary to German eighteenth-century practice the tonal groups were never, at least in theory, mixed at any time during the history of the instrument.

The two schools differed even more in tonal character. The

French 'montre' was generally more foundational and fluty than the German principal; and in the *plein jeu* the quint ranks (unlike those of the Germans) were slightly subordinate to the unisons in power, producing an altogether milder chorus colouring. The seventeenth-century French *plein jeu* had a fairly restrained, silvery quality. But by the late eighteenth century the use of wider scales and higher wind-pressures (up to $3\frac{1}{2}$ or 4 in) had greatly increased the power and breadth of the choruses, though they never approached the forcefulness of the German school.

Unlike the German, the French mutation series consisted entirely of wide-scale flutes, the tone of which tended to merge more readily in the synthetic resultants than that of the narrow-scale sesquialteras. The basis of the series were the bourdons: often wide-scale chimney flutes, made of metal in all but the extreme basses. In tone they were generally more foundational and sombre than the German Rohrflöten, but no less beautiful. The 2 ft of the series, the quarte de nasard, was so named because it sounded a fourth above the nasard, and in order to distinguish it from the doublette 2 ft which belonged to the *plein jeu*.

The outstanding feature of the French organs, however, was undoubtedly their reed choruses which were unparalleled in quality by those of any other country, except perhaps Spain and Portugal. The trompettes and clairons were very powerful and free in tone and the basses had a remarkable roundness coupled with a very prompt attack. The reeds were not supposed to be drawn with the flue-work, with two exceptions. First, it was the practice to draw a cornet and prestant with the reed chorus to reinforce the weak trebles which were outweighed by the enormous basses. This effect was known as 'le grand jeu'. Second, the prestant was usually drawn with the solo trompette or cromorne to cover up irregularities which were more notice-able in solo use. Other solo reeds were the voix humaine, the only representative of the regal family to be found in French organs, and the hautbois, the latter always appearing in a short compass division.

To see how the French seventeenth- and eighteenth-century organs were used we have only to look to the highly stylized and sophisticated music of the period.* The required registration is frequently stated precisely. Pieces are often named after the registration: e.g., *Caprice sur les Grands Jeux, Plein Jeu, Recit de Nasard, Basse et Dessus de Trompette ou de Cornet separe,* and so on. Many of these pieces, for all their musical ingenuity, fail utterly to come to life if they are not performed on the prescribed sonorities.

Details of traditional registrational practice are given by Dom Bedos de Celles in *L'Art du facteur d'Orgues.* This was a remarkably detailed, authoritative and beautifully illustrated work on the construction of the eighteenth-century French organ and its use, written between 1766 and 1778. Dom Bedos says that his suggestions for registration were 'read, examined, corrected and approved by the most celebrated and able organists of Paris, such as Messieurs Calvière, Fouquet, Couperin, Balbastre, and others'. Paraphrased below are some of the more significant examples.

Plein jeu

All the montres, open 8 ft stops, all bourdons, prestants, doublettes, fournitures, cymbales both on the grand orgue and positif. The manuals may be coupled. On the pedals all the trompettes and clairons *or* the flue stops. The *plein jeu* should be treated 'with great flights of harmony, interwoven with art of syncopation, striking discords, suspensions and new harmonic devices'. The *plein jeu* of the positif needs 'clear' playing.

Grand jeu

The cornet, prestant, and all the trompettes and clairons of the grand orgue. Similar registration for the positif which should be coupled. Pedale as for the *plein jeu.*

* Principal composers: Nicholas Gigault (1624–1707); François Couperin (1668–1733); Nicholas de Grigny (1671–1703); Louis Nicholas Clérambault (1676–1738).

Grand jeu de tierce
   Foundation stops from 32 ft* up to nasard, tierce and quarte de nasard 2 ft, but not the doublette 2 ft.

Tierce en taille (a tenor solo tierce effect).
   Accompaniment on two or three 8 ft stops on the grand orgue and pedale flue-work. Solo (to be 'singing' and 'ornamented with taste') on the positif—two 8 ft stops, 4 ft flute, nasard, tierce, quarte and larigot.

Cromorne en taille
   Accompaniment as above. Solo on positif cromorne and prestant.

Solo trompette
   Accompaniment as above. Use the trompette alone, or if the tone is not good, add the prestant.

Voix humaine Solo
   To the voix humaine add bourdon 8 ft, flute 4 ft, and perhaps a prestant or nasard. The tremulant may be added if it is a good one.

Basse de trompette
   Grand orgue: prestant, trompettes and clairons. Positif: two 8 ft, doublette 2 ft and larigot $1\frac{1}{3}$ ft.

For a Duo
   (a) Grand orgue (left hand): *grand jeu de tierce*. Positif (right hand): similar ingredients.
   (b) Right hand: cornet (récit). Left hand: prestant and cromorne (positif).
   (c) Right hand: cornet (récit). Left hand: prestant and cromorne (positif).
   (d) Right hand: trompette (récit). Left hand: *jeu de tierce* (positif).

* There was a montre 32 ft in the grand orgue of the organ at St. Sulpice, Paris, built by Cliquot in 1781 to the design of Dom Bedos.

Historical Background

For a Trio on Two Manuals and Pedals
- (a) i Cornet (récit)
  - ii Cromorne and prestant (positif)
  - iii *Jeu de tierce* (pedale).*
- (b) i Cornet (récit)
  - ii *Jeu de tierce* (positif)
  - iii *Jeu de tierce* or flutes 16 ft, 8 ft, and 4 ft (pedale).
- (c) i Trompette (récit or grand)
  - ii 8 ft flute 4 ft and nasard (positif)
  - iii Pedale as above.
- (d) i *Jeu de tierce* (positif)
  - ii Two flue 8 ft (grand)
  - iii Pedale as above.

For a Slow and Grave Fugue

Grand orgue: prestant, all trompettes and clairons. Positif (coupled): trompette, clairon and cromorne. Pedale: as for *plein jeu*. Do not add cornet or tremulant.

For a Quick Fugue

Use *grand jeu* or *grand jeu de tierce* (manuals coupled). Do not in the latter case add clairon to grand orgue or cromorne to positif.

To Accompany a Choir of Voices or to play Plainsong Melodies

With a large choir use the *plein jeu* and a pedal bass of trompettes and clairons. With several voices in harmony use all the 8 ft stops; with weak voices the 8 ft of the positif only. The voice should always dominate and the accompaniment should serve only to sustain and embellish. To play a plainsong melody, play the theme solemnly on the pedal reeds to which may be added the pedal bombarde 16 ft where there is one. Accompany on the *plein jeux* of grand orgue and positif coupled.

* Here Dom Bedos envisages an abnormally large pedal division containing flute mutations of the 16 ft series. A *Jeu de tiérce à la pédale* means the addition of a nasard 5⅓ ft, quart de nasard 4 ft and tierce 3⅕ ft to foundation stops 16 ft and 8 ft, i.e., a cornet of 16 ft pitch.

The Italian School

The Italian school is entirely different from the French and German and had a longer existence than either. The Italians, having developed their peculiar version of the instrument quite early in the fifteenth century, quickly lost interest in it, so that it was allowed to remain in a comparatively primitive state until well into the nineteenth century. This is not surprising when it is considered that in spite of outstanding keyboard composers such as Merulo, the Gabriellis, Frescobaldi, and Domenico Scarlatti, the Italians were never primarily interested in keyboard music. Their harpsichords, beautiful as they are, never reached the advanced level of the French and Germans. And even though the pianoforte was developed by the Italian Cristofori early in the eighteenth century, it was soon abandoned and left to the Germans and British, each in their own way, to bring it to perfection.

The Italian organ rarely had more than one manual and seldom independent pedals, though an octave of rudimentary pull-downs was quite usual. It consisted of a diapason chorus based on a gentle-toned unison of which all the ranks (unisons and quints only) drew separately. Small organs were complete up to 1 ft; larger ones up to the thirty-sixth $\frac{1}{4}$ ft. There was also a 4 ft flute and sometimes a piffare or a voce umana (not to be confused with the reed stop) which were mild undulating stops of flute and principal tone respectively. Reeds only appeared in the nineteenth century, and then rarely.

Many early Italian organs are to be found in Bologna and Bresnia, the home of the Antegnati family who were distinguished organ builders throughout several generations. The best known is Costanzo Antegnati who, in 1608, published *L'Arte Organica* which gives the specifications of several important organs and hints for their use. One of these is of the organ at Bresnia Cathedral, given below. The Italian stop names are translated into their approximate English equivalents.

103

Historical Background

1. Principale	Open diapason I	8 ft
2. Principale soprano e pedale	Open diapason II (treble & pedal)	8
3. Ottava	Octave	4
4. Decimaquinta	Fifteenth	2
5. Decimanona	Nineteenth	$1\frac{1}{3}$
6. Vigesimaseconda	Twenty-second	1
7. Vigesimasesta	Twenty-sixth	$\frac{2}{3}$
8. Vigesimanono	Twenty-ninth	$\frac{1}{2}$
9. Trigesmaterza	Thirty-third	$\frac{1}{3}$
10. Altra vigesima seconda (larga)	Twenty-second II	1
11. Flauto in decimaquinta	Flageolet	2
12. Flauto in ottava	Octave flute	4

It appears that in this organ and many others the manual compass went down to 16 ft CCC, so that the pitch of the diapason chorus might logically be given as 16 ft, the octave flute as 8 ft and so on.

Apparently the principale soprano e pedale had its treble played from the manual and bass from the pedals. Antegnati's hints for registration give a good indication of how an organ of this kind was used:

(1) For *ripieno* (i.e., a full diapason chorus): open diapason I, octave, fifteenth, nineteenth, twenty-second I, twenty-sixth, twenty-ninth and thirty-third. The normal combination to begin and end with.

(2) For *mezzo ripieno* (half-chorus): open diapason, octave, twenty-ninth, thirty-third, octave flute.

(3) Open diapason, octave, octave flute.

(4) Open diapason and octave flute.

(5) Octave, nineteenth, twenty-second II, octave flute.

(6) Octave and octave flute. For 'divisions' (quick-moving variations) and *canzoni alla francese.*

(7) Octave and octave flute with tremulant. This last should not be added for divisions: one hears it so used sometimes, but it is a confusing and tasteless practice.

(8) Diapason I, alone. A very delicate effect used by Costanzo himself at the Elevation.

(9) Open diapasons I and II together.

(10) Octave flute alone.

(11) Flute and open diapason II. One can begin with both stops on the manual, then descend past the break in the open diapason so as to have a dialogue between flute and pedal.

(12) Open diapason and flageolet, with or without octave. For divisions.

Another work, *Il Transilvano* by Girolamo Diruta, first printed in 1609, endorses the methods of combining the stops given by Antegnati, and gives, among other information, appropriate registrations for the various characters attributed to the ecclesiastical modes.

It is clear that the interest of organists was mainly centred upon the various possibilities of combining the various ranks of the diapason chorus. The mutation ranks were not used melodically as were the French and German solo mutations. They were simply a split-up mixture, each rank breaking down an octave when it reached $1\frac{1}{2}$ inch C. The use of the principale for the contemplative music at the Elevation (cf. Frescobaldi's *Toccata per I'Elevazione*) indicates that the delicate tone of these stops was far removed from the often forceful open diapasons of the modern British organ. Nevertheless, the cumulative effect of the full chorus was quite brilliant and powerful.

The Spanish School

The Spanish school of organ building need only be briefly mentioned here. It is no denigration to say that in modern times it is significant more for what it led to than for what it was, or for the school of composition that it encouraged.

Organs of two or more manuals were common, but pedals were rare and generally only pull-downs. Flue choruses were generally after the Italian pattern, except that the higher pitches frequently appeared together as many-ranked mixtures. But completely unlike the Italians, from early times Spanish organs were rich in reed choruses of tremendous stridency, the impact of which was enhanced by the pipes being projected horizontally from the fronts of the organ cases. It was in Spain, too, that the swell box was first introduced in the early eighteenth century. Cavaillé-Coll is said to have been much influenced by the Spanish reed choruses the effect of which he strove to incorporare in his reed-dominated 'symphonic' organs; and Father Willis was greatly influenced by Cavaillé-Coll. Since the British reed-dominated full swell stems to some extent from Willis, the modern British organ owes much, for better or worse, to the Spanish organs of the eighteenth century or carlier.

The Nineteenth Century in Europe

After 1800 or so the impetus to build classical organs petered out because they no longer satisfied contemporary musical taste. Up to at least 1750 in Germany and France the organ was regarded as pre-eminent among instruments. Foremost composers, demanding no subtlety of expression from the organ that it was unable to give, wrote their best music for it. After about 1750 musical interest turned to the development of other media such as the orchestra and the pianoforte which were more amenable to the new artistic demands. In consequence, organ works by the musical giants of the nineteenth century became the exception rather than the rule and of small significance compared with their main output. Compared with the wealth of pre-1750 organ literature, only a few dozen compositions by Haydn, Mozart, Mendelssohn, Brahms, Franck and Liszt—and at the end of the century the prodigious output of Reger—stand out from a mass of mediocrity.

Most nineteenth-century musicians were not interested in the authentic performance of earlier music. If the organ was to

VII. A handsome Victorian console with flat drawstop jambs and
trigger swell pedal (not shown); provided by Gray & Davison Ltd
for the eighteenth-century organ at St Mary, Rotherhithe in *c*. 1870.

survive, therefore, it had to copy as best it could the dynamics of the nineteenth-century orchestra—the ability to produce a gradual *crescendo* and *diminuendo* and to change and blend tone colours effortlessly in an orchestral manner. In other words, it had to become 'romantic' or 'symphonic'. The first organ builder to achieve this was the French Aristide 'Cavaillé-Coll (1811–1899), the undoubted father of the romantic organ.

Cavaillé-Coll introduced an entirely new conception of the organ and installed his first fully-developed example in St Denis Abbey, near Paris, in 1841. Shortly afterwards a government contract enabled him to impose his conception in many French cathedrals where old organs had been allowed to fall into dilapidation.

No single Cavaillé-Coll specification can be quoted as entirely typical; but the organ at Ste Clotilde, Paris, is characteristic, and has been little altered from its original state. It is famous because César Franck, probably the greatest composer to be inspired by the Cavaillé-Coll organ, was its first organist, from 1859 to 1890.

STE CLOTILDE, PARIS: ORGAN BY CAVAILLÉ-COLL

GRAND ORGUE Man. I		POSITIF Man. II	
Montre	16	Bourdon	16
Bourdon	16	Montre	8
Montre	8	Gambe	8
Gambe	8	Flûte harmonique	8
Flûte harmonique	8	Bourdon	8
Bourdon	8	Salicional	8
Prestant	4	Prestant	4
Octave	4	Flûte octaviante	4
Quinte	$2\frac{2}{3}$	Quinte	$2\frac{2}{3}$
Doublette	2	Doublette	2
Plein jeu	V	Plein jeu	IV
Bombarde	16	Clarinette	8
Trompette	8	Trompette	8
Clairon	4	Clairon	4

I

RECIT EXPRESSIF (enclosed) Man. III		PEDALE	
Bourdon	8	Quintaton	32
Flûte harmonique	8	Contrebasse	16
Viole de gambe	8	Flûte	8
Voix céleste	8	Octave	4
Flûte octaviante	4	Bombarde	16
Octavin	2	Basson	16
Basson-hautbois	8	Trompette	8
Trompette	8	Clairon	4
Clairon	4		
Tremblant		14 Pedales de combinaison	

Cavaillé-Coll's manual divisions had no separate identity: they existed mainly for ease of registration and merely combined to form a massive *grand choeur*. Often the grand orgue was the only division to possess chorus upperwork. The foundation flue-work was a blend of montres, flutes, and strings, forming a composite diapason tone of moderate power and much beauty. Cavaillé-Coll's montre was a rather stringy open diapason, and he was an innovator in developing pure-toned harmonic flutes and moderate string tones with a quasi-orchestral flavour. The mixtures could be drawn with the flue foundation, but were thought of more as adjuncts to the powerful, free-toned reed choruses which completely dominated the entire organ after the manner of orchestral brass. These were voiced on low pressure, but Cavaillé-Coll kept up the power of the trebles in a novel way by putting them on a slightly higher wind pressure than the basses. He also used harmonic (double-length) tubes, and disposed his more powerful trompettes 'en chamade' in Spanish style.

With the exception of an occasional cornet, solo mutations formed no part of the Cavaillé-Coll organ. Only through the scholarly intervention of Guilmant and Saint-Saens was he persuaded to include some in his later schemes for the proper performance of early music.

In order that his organs could be used symphonically Cavaillé-Coll devised a special system of control. The stops of each division were planted on two ventil chests, one containing the flue stops up to 2 ft (fonds) and the other the reeds and mixtures (jeux de combinaison). The ventils were controlled by hitch-down pedals, as were the inter-divisional and octave couplers. A composition calling for a series of *crescendi* and *diminuendi* was registered by preparing the stops in advance, and then playing on the grand orgue throughout, adding or withdrawing sections of the organ as required by means of the pedal-operated ventils and couplers.

Oddly enough, Cavaillé-Coll never really took to the swell box, being content to enclose only the recit expressif, even in a five-manual organ. No doubt he realized that even at its best the swell box produces only a very artificial form of crescendo, and he preferred to rely on the more natural crescendo obtained by adding groups of stops.

Because the heavier wind-pressures and multiplicity of couplers of the Cavaillé-Coll system would have made tracker action impracticable, he adopted the excellent Barker lever action and brought it to a remarkable degree of efficiency.

The Cavaillé-Coll organ remained the standard French instrument until well into the twentieth century. His organs were so well made that many survive, little altered, until the present day. For the most part they are utterly unsuitable for seventeenth- and eighteenth-century music because they lack the tonal balances, transparency and solo sonorities that such music requires. No one could have been more misguided than Widor when he wrote 'after Cavaillé-Coll came the proper playing of the works of Bach'. Nevertheless they fully met the needs of a vital school of composition of which Franck, Widor, Guilmant and Vierne are perhaps the most illustrious, and whose music in original editions is registered in detail in terms of the Cavaillé-Coll organ.

The nineteenth-century organ in Germany followed very

much after the ideals of Cavaillé-Coll; but by retaining a basis of classical design it was, in practice, of much wider general utility. The German organs were often large and unwieldy. For symphonic expression they relied at first on ventils, but later on the 'Rollschweller' stop-crescendo, a device particularly useful for achieving the orchestral-style dynamics demanded by the organ works of composers such as Liszt, Reubke, Karg-Elert and Reger.

The Organ Reform Movement

The organ reform movement, or the 'Classical Revival', or the 'Baroque Revival', began in Germany in the 1920s. It resulted in a return to the principles of the seventeenth and eighteenth-century organ builders.

By about 1914 there was a growing dissatisfaction among thinking musicians with the romantic organ as a medium for the interpretation of early music, and the advances of musicology had led to a demand for a more authentic approach to the problems of performance. It was thus inevitable that interest should turn again to the seventeenth- and eighteenth-century organs, many of which had survived in little altered condition—more through lack of money to 'improve' them than for any other reason. These organs were closely studied and restored, and their principles of construction (including the work-disposition and tracker action) were incorporated in new instruments. A landmark was the construction of a small organ at Freiburg University by Dr Oskar Walcker in 1921 in accordance with details given by Pretorius in his *Syntagma*. This pioneer instrument was designed by Willibald Gurlitt, one of the protagonists of the movement. Shortly afterwards the publication in facsimile editions of the invaluable source works of Praetorius, Dom Bedos, Mattheson, Adlung and Werckmeister added immensely to popular knowledge and the possibilities of studying old instruments and their use. The movement also brought about a reform in the performance style of early

110

music, both in terms of registration and details of phrasing and articulation. In 1926, Karl Straube, organist of the Thomas-kirche, Leipzig, and one of the most distinguished performers of the day, took the opportunity of correcting the romantic dynamic markings he had inserted in his editions of old German masters in 1904. He even re-edited Reger, with the composer's approval, in terms of the classical organ. Some of the new organs of this period were severely 'neo-baroque' in style, un-compromising in their return to the seventeenth century with no romantic concessions, either by way of tone-colours or mechanical aids to registration. Other organs were more eclectic in conception, it being realized that the needs of schools of composition outside the seventeenth and eighteenth centuries should properly be catered for.

The movement quickly spread to Holland, Scandinavia, France and the USA, and by 1939 had gained a firm hold in these countries. Only in Britain was the movement slow to take root, and not until the 1950s did it make any significant impact. But this was hardly surprising. Throughout her organ history, Britain has always been slow to learn from foreign countries, though once a start has been made her progress has invariably been rapid. This will become clear as we now turn to our brief survey of the history and use of the British organ.

The British School

In studying the British school of organ building our main concern—for essential back-ground knowledge of the instru-ments and their use—will be the period of the school of native composers extending from John Redford to Samuel Wesley, roughly 1540 to 1800. An unavoidable dividing line in British organ history is the Commonwealth, because it was then that the growing antipathy of several decades of puritanism finally succeeded in banning the organ as a church instrument and brought about a temporary cessation of the organ building craft.

111

Until the nineteenth century the British school was slow to develop. It is safe to say that no organ had pedals until the 1720s; even then they were rudimentary and slow to gain acceptance. Not until the 1840s were there organs with manual and pedal compasses on which the works of J. S. Bach could be performed as written; but from thence onwards development was continuous and rapid. It is, of course, only by comparison with the advanced north German school that the pre-1840 British organs are found wanting. The French, Spanish and Italian schools, each in their own way, were equally limited. The British wanted none of the north German brilliance and drama and, like the Italians, found their own modest instruments entirely adequate for their needs.

The Pre-Commonwealth Period

The pre-Commonwealth period can be dealt with quite briefly because comparatively little is known about it: only one small complete organ and a small quantity of pipework has survived. But there is sufficient evidence to show that organs were small, and without pedals, and before the beginning of the seventeenth century never possessed more than one keyboard. It is likely that from the time of Henry VIII Italian influences were at work, since he is known to have introduced Italian craftsmen of all kinds and almost all surviving stringed instruments are Italian. The stop list of the small organ built by Thomas Dallam for Eton College in 1613, for example, has much in common with typical small Italian organs of the same period:

ETON COLLEGE: ORGAN BY THOMAS DALLAM, 1613

1.	Stopped diapason	8 ft
2.	Principal	4
3.	Flute	4
4.	Octavo	2
5.	Fifteenth	2

All the pipes were of tin. The octavo was presumably a second fifteenth, Italian style.

The earliest recorded specification of a two-manual organ is of the one built by Thomas Dallam for Worcester Cathedral in 1613–1614 to the design of Thomas Tomkins:

WORCESTER CATHEDRAL: TWO-MANUAL ORGAN BY THOMAS DALLAM, 1613–1614

GREAT ORGAN

1. Open diapason I	(metal)	8 ft
2. Open diapason II	(metal)	8
3. Principal I	(metal)	4
4. Principal II	(metal)	4
5. Twelfth	(metal)	$2\frac{2}{3}$
6. Fifteenth I	(metal)	2
7. Fifteenth II	(metal)	2
8. Recorder	(stopped metal)	8

CHAIR ORGAN

9. Stopped diapason	(wood)	8
10. Principal	(metal)	4
11. Fifteenth	(metal)	2
12. Two and twentieth	(metal)	1
13. Flute	(stopped wood)	4

By contemporary standards this was a large and complete organ. The separate twenty-second and the absence of compound stops and reeds all point to Italian influence. The tonal character of the organs of this period must be largely conjectural, but it is interesting to note that the quality most admired by contemporary observers was 'sweetness'. There is no mention of brilliance or power; and it is hardly to be supposed that such qualities would be evident in organs without chorus mixtures and scarcely any upperwork above 2 ft pitch. Even so, it does not necessarily follow that the cumulative effect of the seven great organ diapason ranks at Worcester was insignificant, though the liveliness that only mixtures can give could have formed no part of it.

The second manual, the 'chair' organ was the counterpart of the European positive and originated in much the same way. It was so-called either because of its occasional position near or behind the organist's seat or chair; or, as Dr Sumner has observed, because it was a subsidiary organ that took a *turn* or was *turned to* in contrast to the larger one.* The word 'chair', signifying one who helps or takes a turn, occurs frequently in seventeenth-century English, and various derivations survive in modern usage (e.g., chore, *char*woman). Only later was 'chair organ' corrupted into 'choir organ'; not the reverse as has been frequently and erroneously stated. Where the chair organ was placed in a separate case behind the seat (as at Worcester) it was the equivalent of the German Rückpositiv, and was similarly a 4 ft organ as opposed to the 8 ft foundation of the great.

A two-manual organ of this kind was known as a 'double' organ, partly but not entirely because it was two organs in one. The term 'double' was applied to the great and 'single' to the choir. This was a continuation of pre-seventeenth-century usage when only single-manual organs were known in Britain: the terms 'double' and 'single' indicated the foundation pitch or compass and were consequently applied to organs of 8 ft and 4 ft pitch respectively.

We have no more evidence of the way the pre-Commonwealth organs were used than of how they sounded. There are no treatises of instruction and with one or two exceptions, the prolific body of known pre-Commonwealth organ music is devoid of hints for registration. One exception is the group of voluntaries composed specifically for a double organ with two manuals in which the manual changes are indicated in the scores.† These interesting pieces were clearly composed to exploit the resources of an organ of the Worcester type. They consist of a series of left-hand solos on the great (or 'double') organ accompanied on the chair (alternatively referred to as the

* W. L. Sumner, *The Organ, Its Evolution, Principles of Construction and Use* (1952), 3rd edn., London, 1962, pp. 161–163.

† John Lugge, *Three Voluntaries for Double Organ,* ed. Susi Jeans and John Steele, Novello (1955). Lugge was organist of Exeter Cathedral from at least 1602 until 1645 or later.

'single', 'tenor' or 'little' organ), both hands moving to the great for a final section. One can imagine that the broader 'double' tones of the great would have contrasted effectively with the softer but brighter tones of the 'single' chair; and that the contrast would have been intensified by the different placing of the two divisions.

The Restoration Period until 1800

From the restoration period onwards there emerges a much clearer picture of the British organ and its use. Enough pipework and written evidence survives to enable us to judge how the organs sounded; moreover, Restoration composers begin to specify their registrational requirements, and their eighteenth-century successors, like their French contemporaries, usually state them precisely.*

For a short time after 1660 a few of the older organ makers, principally the Dallam family, resumed work on pre-Commonwealth lines. But it was not long before British organ building received a new infusion of life at the hands of two rival craftsmen, or families of craftsmen, who came (or returned) to this country after a European sojourn during the Commonwealth. They were ('Father') Bernard Smith (*c.* 1628–1708) who came from Germany or Holland, and the Harris family consisting of Thomas Harris (*d.* 1685) and his son Renatus (1652–1724) who came from France. Smith and the Harrises introduced into the British organ chorus mixtures, the solo cornet, and solo and chorus reeds. British organists and composers were prepared to accept these developments, though they still had no use for pedals. The stop list of the organ built by Smith in 1680 for Christ Church Cathedral, Oxford, though modest enough by modern standards, shows the considerable advance on, say, the Worcester organ of 1614:†

---

* Principal composers for the British organ 1660–1800: J. Blow (1649–1695); H. Purcell (1658–1695); W. Croft (1678–1727); M. Green (1710–1779); J. Stanley (1713–1786); W. Walond (1725–1770).
† See p. 113.

Historical Background

CHRIST CHURCH CATHEDRAL, OXFORD: ORGAN
BY BERNARD SMITH, 1680

GREAT ORGAN

1.	Open diapason	8 ft
2.	Stopped diapason	8
3.	Principal	4
4.	Twelfth	$2\frac{2}{3}$
5.	Fifteenth	2
6.	Tierce	$1\frac{3}{5}$
7.	Sesquialtera	III
8.	Cornet (from middle C)	IV
9.	Trumpet	8

CHOIR ORGAN

10.	Stopped diapason	8
11.	Principal	4
12.	Flute	4
13.	Fifteenth	2

Compass: GG (short octave) to c, 50 notes.*

The great sesquialtera was a diapason chorus mixture almost
certainly containing the tierce, in accordance with Smith's
normal practice. Until well after 1800 the majority of British
organ builders followed this practice of Smith's, with the result
that their diapason choruses had a strong reedy tang with none
of the purity of the European *plein jeux*. (Even in the nineteenth
and early twentieth centuries this practice persisted, and not
until the classical revival of the 1950s was it completely shaken
off.) Renatus Harris, however, at least sometimes kept some of
his chorus mixtures free of the tierce, making it available
separately.

` Another innovation, first introduced by Smith, was a third
manual called the 'echo organ'. This was a short-compass semi-
solo division, after the style of the French récit, rarely extending

* Actually from GGG (see p. 34). The 'short octave' was a space and
money-saving system in which the bass compass was extended by sub-
stituting longer pipes for unnecessary notes. The keyboard ostensibly
extended to BBB, but in fact the CC sharp and BBB keys sounded AAA
and GGG respectively.

below fiddle G. It was placed in a completely and permanently closed box in order to subdue the tone. An important event occurred in 1712 when Abraham Jordan, at St Magnus-the-Martyr, London Bridge, provided the box with a sliding pedal-controlled shutter, thereby inventing the swell box which, it will be recalled, was at about this time being developed independently in Spain. Despite its crudity, the expression obtainable from this device appealed greatly to the taste of British organists. From thence onwards the third manual was nearly always a short compass swell. By the end of the century the swell, with extended compass, had grown so much in importance that it began to supersede the choir organ as the principal secondary division.

During the eighteenth century any resemblance to the Continental work-disposition was soon abandoned, the divisions being for the most part disposed within a single main case. Specifications settled down to a fairly consistent and conventional pattern, varying only in points of detail. Probably the best example that can be quoted is that of the organ built at St Mary, Rotherhithe in 1764 by John Byfield junior, a grandson of Renatus Harris. The greater part of this splendid organ survives today in restored condition and is of immense value in reconstructing contemporary registration. Here is the original specification:

ST MARY, ROTHERHITHE: ORGAN BY JOHN BYFIELD, 1764

GREAT ORGAN

1.	Open diapason	8
2.	Stopped diapason	8
3.	Principal	4
4.	Nason	4
5.	Twelfth	$2\frac{2}{3}$
6.	Fifteenth	2
7.	Sesquialtera	IV
8.	Cornet (middle C)	V
9.	Trumpet	8
10.	Clarion	4

CHOIR ORGAN

11.	Stopped diapason	8
12.	Principal	4
13.	Flute	4
14.	Fifteenth	2
15.	Vox humana	8

SWELL ORGAN

16.	Open diapason	8
17.	Stopped diapason	8
18.	Principal	4
19.	Cornet	III
20.	Trumpet	8
21.	Hautboy	8

Compass: Great and choir: GG (short octave) to e, 54 notes
Swell: fiddle G to e, 34 notes

The tonal individuality of the late seventeenth-century and eighteenth-century organs naturally differed from one maker to another, and the instruments of the mid-eighteenth-century builders are generally more sophisticated than those of their predecessors. Even so, apart from the development of the swell organ, there was little essential difference between the musical scope of an organ built in 1685 and one a century later. It is consequently possible to give a generalized outline of the tonal character of the British organ during the period we are now considering.

The main diapason chorus on the great was clear and sprightly, and was founded on a fairly bright but gentle 8 ft stop above which the chorus was erected in ranks of more or less equal volume. The usually present chorus tierce added a strong reedy tang. Often, as at Rotherhithe, the chorus was extremely bold and vital; but without the many-ranked quint mixtures of the German school it could in no sense compete with the latter in forcefulness, brilliance or purity. There was no deliberate division into wide and narrow-scale groups. The stopped diapasons, usually of wood and of medium scale, were more perky than the European Gedeckts and bourdons. They were intended to be drawn with the diapasons and to add body to the chorus. An eighteenth-century chorus without the stopped diapasons does, in fact, sound remarkably thin.

The quality of the chorus reeds varied more than the flue-work. But at their best, like the superb great trumpet at Rother-hithe, they had a fine brilliant tone—more restrained and 'British' than the French reeds—which blended well, and coloured and enriched the flue chorus without swamping it.

The cornets were narrower in scale than the French but no less telling. When 'mounted' above the great soundboard, as they often were, they sang out prominently and were a favourite solo effect, both for running 'cornet voluntaries' and for giving out psalm and hymn tunes.

The choir organ was a kind of lesser great of smaller scale and normally based on 4 ft pitch. Since it rarely contained upperwork above 2 ft and never any solo mutations it was by no means on a par with the European positive divisions, and it never equalled the full great in volume. Often it contained the only 4 ft flute in the organ. There was usually an 8 ft solo reed, normally a cremona. This was a somewhat milder version of the Krummhorn or cromorne, but much bolder and more interesting than the modern organ clarinet.

The swell organ, as has been explained, developed from the boxed echo. One use of the swell was to provide, with the box closed, the echoed solos which the music of the period frequently demands. For instance, there are many places in the voluntaries of Stanley and Green where a solo on the great trumpet or cornet was required to be echoed by a similar sonority on the swell. The swell organ was also used to provide quiet 'expressive' effects within the limits of its compass, left-hand work below fiddle G being played on the great or choir stopped diapasons.

A good idea of the conventional use of these organs can be obtained from the instructions of composers and the treatises of Blewitt and Marsh published during the last decade of the eighteenth century.* The following is a sample of typical combinations taken from the works of late seventeenth and eighteenth-century composers:

Typical Late Seventeenth- and Eighteenth-Century Combinations†
>   Full organ (sometimes qualified by 'without the trumpet' or 'with the trumpet').

Diapasons
Diapason and flute
Diapasons and principal
Corno or diapasons
Stop diapason
Flute
Cornet
Sesquialtera
Trumpet
Vox Humana
Hautboy
Swell
Echoes

'Full organ' did not mean all the stops in the organ (indeed, this was not possible since there were no couplers); nor even necessarily full great. It simply meant a *full* great organ effect, comprising perhaps great up to one or two mixtures with or without reeds. The cornet was purely a solo stop, forming no part of the full organ.

Contrary to modern usage, 'diapasons' referred to both open and stopped diapasons 8 ft. These were nearly always drawn together and were regarded equally as the 'foundation of the organ'. The 'stop diapason' was often used alone; the open diapason rarely. The full tones of the stopped diapason were usually needed to fill out the open stop and to disguise the sluggish speech of its bass pipes conveyanced off in the front of

* John Marsh, *Eighteen Voluntaries for the Organ ... To which is prefix'd an Explanation of the ... Stops etc.*, Preston & Son, London, 1791.

Jonas Blewitt, *A Complete Treatise on the Organ to which is added a set of Explanatory Voluntaries etc.*, Longman & Broderip, London, 1795.

† See also the paragraphs below.

the case. 'Diapason and flute' meant the stopped (not the open) diapason and flute 4 ft. 'Diapasons and principal' required open and stopped diapasons to be drawn with the principal. The latter was never used alone; indeed, with the occasional exception of the open diapason in *sostenuto* passages, the only stops supposed to be drawn singly were the stopped diapason, the 4 ft flute (see below) and the dulciana.

With one exception it was customary to include a stopped diapason (often an open diapason as well) in all solo effects, cornet, trumpet, hautboy, vox humana etc, both to give them body and to cover up any tonal irregularities. The exception was the flute 4 ft, and flute solos were consequently intended to sound an octave higher than written. 'Sesquialtera' required the chorus stop of that name to be used solo in the lower register in combination with suitable 8 ft and 4 ft stops—an effect not unlike the French 'tierce en taille'. As the sesquialtera usually broke to 12, 15, 17 above middle C, it was used with the stopped diapason and principal as a substitute cornet when the latter was not available.

Eighteenth-century composers were very fond of imitating orchestral instruments on the organ, not least the horns. A French horn stop (a rather thick-toned trumpet) was sometimes provided; but when this was not available the diapasons, which sounded quite horn-like in their middle register, were considered to be an effective substitute: hence the instruction 'corno or diapasons'.

The terms 'echo' and 'swell' indicated two different uses of the swell organ. In the former instance it was to be used with box closed in the style of the older echo organ, as described above. The latter term was applied to quieter movements in voluntaries where the expression of the swell box was intended to be fully applied.

It is clear that, in common with the French and German practice, registration was pre-arranged, and there are no indications that a stop 'build up' was required during performance.

British registration of this period was clearly conservative and unadventurous. No upperwork was drawn without a firm basis of foundation tone. The modern, supposedly 'baroque' practice of using 2 ft stops and mixtures with a single stopped diapason would probably have been regarded with horror. Apart from the cornet and solo sesquialtera there is no suggestion of synthetic tone-building; nor any hint that the chorus reeds and cornet should ever be used in the style of the French *grand jeu.*

The Nineteenth Century

During the first two or three decades of the nineteenth century the state of the British organ was confused and archaic. The general tonal character of the eighteenth-century organ continued well into the new century; but with the swell organ sometimes extended to full compass and the dubious advantages of an octave or so of 'pull down' pedals connected to 'pedal pipes' of large-scale open wood and ponderous tone. These pedal features were introduced tardily during the eighteenth century; but they made little impression on our organists who preferred the sonority obtainable by hand from the long manual compasses. Even as late as 1851 the seventy-five years old Sir George Smart (who had played at the coronations of William IV and Victoria) when asked to try an organ with pedals, replied, 'My dear sir, I have never in my life played upon a *grid-iron.*' In 1860 the Lichfield Cathedral organist, Spofforth, referring to a fine ten stop pedal organ then provided by Holdich, said, 'You may put them there, but I shall never use them.'

For the most part eighteenth-century pedal attachments can hardly have been used other than for improvisation and accompaniment. Only by the time of Samuel Wesley and William Russell was an obbligato pedal part specified; it was then a kind of 'third hand' helping the manuals out occasionally and confined mainly to pedal points or to fairly slow-moving passages.

The position was such that Mendelssohn during his early London visits (the first was in 1829) found no organs on which J. S. Bach's organ works could be properly played. That this

VIII. Organ at the Marienkirche, Lübeck, 1516–18. This drawing from
Dr A. G. Hill's famous *Organ Cases of the Middle Ages and
Renaissance* illustrates the early 'work principle' arrangement of great
and back-positive organs.

situation was remedied and British organ building set on the
right lines was due to the organ builder William Hill (1789–
1870) and Dr Henry John Gauntlett (1805–1876). Nowadays
Gauntlett is best known as the composer of a few favourite
hymn tunes (notably St Albinus and St George); but he was in
his day a distinguished church musician and a firm advocate of
the 'German' compass (manuals from CC, pedals from CCC)
for which Bach composed. He found a willing ally in Hill who,
under Gauntlett's guidance, built or rebuilt a number of
important organs, notably at St Peter's, Cornhill; Christ
Church, Newgate Street, London; and Ashton-under-Lyne
Parish Church. Mendelssohn played the London organs with
great success during his later visits.

The Hill organ of the 1840s was a tremendous step forward.
For the first time there was a British organ on which all known
organ music could be played instead of the interesting but
extremely limited native school. The specification of the earliest
complete example, built for Great George Street Chapel,
Liverpool, in 1841, is worth studying. The manual compass was
CC to f, 54 notes; the pedals CCC to D, 27 notes.

GREAT GEORGE STREET CHAPEL, LIVERPOOL: ORGAN
BY WILLIAM HILL, 1841
GREAT ORGAN

1. Tenoroon (to T.C.)	16		9. Tenth	$3\frac{3}{5}$
2. Bourdon (from T.C.)	16		10. Twelfth	$2\frac{2}{3}$
3. Open diapason	8		11. Fifteenth	2
4. Open diapason	8		12. Sesquialtera	III
5. Stopped diapason	8		13. Mixture	III
6. Quint	$5\frac{1}{3}$		14. Doublette	II
7. Principal	4		15. Posaune	8
8. Flute	4		16. Clarion	4

SWELL ORGAN

17. Tenoroon (to T.C.)	16	27. Fifteenth	2
18. Bourdon (from T.C.)	16	28. Flageolet	2
19. Open diapason	8	29. Sesquialtera	III
20. Dulciana	8	30. Mixture	II
21. Stopped diapason	8	31. Echo cornet	V
22. Corno flute	8	32. Contra fagotto	16
23. Quint	$5\frac{1}{3}$	33. Cornopean	8
24. Principal	4	34. Trumpet	8
25. Suabe flute	4	35. Oboe	8
26. Twelfth	$2\frac{2}{3}$	36. Clarion	4

CHOIR ORGAN

37. Open diapason	8	42. Stopped flute	4
38. Dulciana	8	43. Oboe flute	4
39. Stopped diapason	8	44. Wald flute	2
40. Clarabella	8	45. Cremona	8
41. Principal	4		

SOLO ORGAN

46. Tuba mirabilis   8

COUPLERS, ETC.	PEDAL ORGAN	
Swell to great	47. Open diapason	16
Choir to great	48. Bourdon	16
Great to pedal	49. Principal	8
Swell to pedal	50. Fifteenth	4
Choir to pedal	51. Sesquialtera	V
Five composition pedals	52. Trombone	16

The mature Hill organ of the 1840s, of which the foregoing specification is an example, contained several classical features in British guise, though there was no attempt to introduce the classical work-disposition of divisions. The great diapason chorus was classically proportioned and rich in upperwork. The classical positive was to some extent present in the swell flue chorus. There were no flute mutations, but the ample diapason mutations and sesquialteras could, in fact, be used effectively in synthetic tone-building by anyone who wished to do so. Hill's pedal scheme, a standard provision in several of his mid-century organs, was remarkably independent and a model disposition within the limits of only six stops. There were also some romantic tendencies which set the pattern of the British organ for years to come. The swell had completely supplanted the choir in importance and acquired a new secondary chorus character—the reed and mixture 'full swell' with the double reed foundation. The choir was relegated to the subordinate role of a miscellaneous solo-accompanimental division with no chorus identity, but still unenclosed. Another innovation was the solo tuba, voiced on heavy pressure to obtain power and tonal purity. Hill did not favour a reed-dominated full organ and at first voiced his chorus reeds on the flue-work light-pressure of 3 to $3\frac{1}{2}$ in. Later, he used chorus reed pressures of up to 5 in, seeking fairly successfully to combine the advantages of heavy wind (strong trebles and stability of tuning) and light wind (prompt basses and ability to blend without overpowering the diapason chorus).

Other mid-century builders, notably Walker, Gray & Davison, Holdich and Nicholson, followed Hill in making a classical type of British organ, and the period has been appropriately described as a 'golden age' of British organ building. Unhappily this halcyon period was short-lived. In the Great Exhibition of 1851 the British public were first acquainted with the work of Henry Willis and a German organ builder, Edmund Schulze, whose innovations in the field of reed and flue voicing respectively were greatly to change the character of the British organ during the second half-century.

Willis was much influenced by Cavaillé-Coll whose concept of the reed-dominated 'grand choeur' he translated into British terms. Willis did this by developing, with the aid of his brother George, a new type of heavy-wind chorus reed, of a restrained tone quality that has come to be regarded as typically British, but of unprecedented power, richness and regularity. At first he followed Cavaillé-Coll in using increased pressures only in the upper part of the compass. Later he used uniform pressures (7 in for chorus reeds and upwards of 15 in for pedal reeds and tubas) preferring to restrain the basses by weighting the tongues, a practice which inevitably diminished their promptness of attack. He also introduced the Cavaillé-Coll type of harmonic flute and string tone and to some extent copied the rather stringy tones of the French diapasons. But although the Willis full great was dominated by the striking grandeur of the reeds, the diapason chorus was always self-sufficient and within classical limits of restraint. His mixtures were always part of the flue chorus. They invariably contained tierces, though not so strong as to be objectionable. From a classical viewpoint the main defect of the Willis concept lay in the swell diapason chorus which was too weak to form a satisfactory positive.

Willis was among the first to realise the importance of the double reed in the full swell, and of providing this important stop in small schemes before a flue double or clarion.

The Willis organ was essentially symphonic, but with a sound chorus basis and no exaggerated sonorities. For its control he developed a superbly prompt and reliable tubular-pneumatic action and a system of adjustable combination pistons. The result was the ideal Victorian church and concert organ, fully adapted to the needs of an age in which nobility of tone, flexibility of control and ability to emulate orchestral dynamics were considered to be of paramount importance. As an example of a typical Willis tonal scheme we cannot do better than quote the specification of the organ he built for St Paul's Cathedral, London in 1872. It formed the model for many subsequent cathedral organs and survives as the nucleus of the present instrument.

St Paul's Cathedral, London: Organ by Henry Willis, 1872

GREAT ORGAN

1.	Double open diapason	16	8.	Octave quint	$2\frac{2}{3}$
2.	Open diapason (large)	8	9.	Fourniture 17, 19, 22	III
3.	Open diapason (small)	8	10.	Mixture 24, 26, 29	III
4.	Claribel flute	8	11.	Trombone	16
5.	Quint	$5\frac{1}{3}$	12.	Tromba	8
6.	Principal	4	13.	Clarion	4
7.	Flûte harmonique	4			

The British School

CHOIR ORGAN

14. Bourdon	16	20. Principal	4
15. Open diapason	8	21. Flûte harmonique	4
16. Dulciana	8	22. Flageolet	2
17. Violoncello	8	23. Cor anglais	8
18. Claribel flute	8	24. Corno di bassetto	8
19. Lieblich Gedeckt	8		

SWELL ORGAN (enclosed)

25. Contra gamba	16	31. Fifteenth	2
26. Open diapason	8	32. Echo cornet 17, 19, 22	III
27. Lieblich Gedeckt	8	33. Contra posaune	16
28. Salicional	8	34. Cornopean	8
29. Vox angelica	8	35. Hautboy	8
30. Principal	4	36. Clarion	4

SOLO ORGAN

37. Flûte harmonique	8	40. Orchestral oboe	8
38. Concert flute	4	41. Tuba magna	8
39. Corno di bassetto	8	42. Clarion	4

PEDAL ORGAN

43. Double open diapason	32
44. Open diapason	16
45. Violone	16
46. Octave	8
47. Violoncello	8
48. Mixture 17, 19, 22	III
49. Contra posaune	32
50. Grand bombarde	16
51. Clarion	8

COUPLERS

Solo to great
Choir to great
Swell octave to great
Swell to great
Swell sub-octave to great
Great to pedal
Swell to pedal
Choir to pedal
Solo to pedal

Wind pressures: flue-work 2½ to 7 in; reeds 3½ to 17½ in.

16 thumb pistons, 4 to each manual.
4 composition pedals to great and pedal.
1 pedal (reversible) for great to pedal.
1 pedal for swell to great.

Manual compass CC to a³, 58 notes. Pedal compass CCC to F, 30 notes.

127

Schulze's British organs numbered far less than those of Willis but his methods were no less influential. He introduced a new kind of diapason chorus based on an 8 ft stop in which maximum power and harmonic development were obtained from a wind-pressure of only 3½ in. On this powerful unison, bolder than anything previously heard in Britain, he erected a chorus of equal-powered ranks culminating in a quint mixture of phenomenal brilliance. The result was a chorus of immense splendour, but too loud to be tolerable except in climaxes. Because of this and the somewhat sluggish attack inherent in the Schulze diapason tone, the chorus was unclear and a poor medium for polyphony. Schulze made beautiful strings and flutes, and charming small-scale Lieblich Gedeckts which were much copied by other builders, including Willis. But he had no use for the full swell, and the overwhelming power of the full great eclipsed the other manual divisions. In short, the Schulze organ was capable of moments of isolated splendour and beautiful soft effects, but it was too rugged to be of more than limited general utility.

The combined influence of Willis and Schulze undermined the classical organ because it unintentionally lent strength to a current musical taste which misunderstood the true purpose of upperwork and regarded mixtures as unpleasant, outmoded survivals. It was thought that the early organ builders provided plentiful mixtures only because they had neither the technique nor the wind supply to make foundation tone of sufficient power and beauty—a view which neglected and untuned upperwork in old organs did nothing to dispel. With the coming of Schulze's powerful diapasons (his upperwork was rejected as being too strident) and Willis's grand reeds, upperwork seemed superfluous. Consequently, towards the end of the century, nearly all organ builders whittled down their upperwork both in quality and in quantity, preferring to concentrate all the power of the organ in a few loud diapasons and reeds. Tonal variety was provided by often beautiful but unblending solo stops, flutes and new kinds of string tone. All divisions except the great and pedals were enclosed. In other words, the debased kind of organ mentioned in our account of the tonal structure of the British organ had arrived.

It was a type of organ, however, that fully satisfied a contemporary taste much preoccupied with choral accompaniment and orchestral transcriptions, and which consequently thought of the organ more and more in orchestral terms. Thus, almost conversely with the decline of upperwork, came a greater emphasis on means of obtaining pseudo-orchestral expression—enclosure, electric action and more efficient means of changing the stops—and the development of an orchestral style of playing which was applied indiscriminately to the current repertoire, regardless of style or historical context.

By 1900 the construction of an organ with anything approaching a classical chorus structure was rare, though a few exceptional examples seem to defy the spirit of the age. The epitome of decadence were the organs of Robert Hope Jones, an eccentric genius and a pioneer in the cause of electric action. He conceived the basically unsound idea that the brilliance of organ tone should derive from the natural harmonics of foundation tone, and tried to put it into effect in a singularly odd manner. Eschewing chorus upperwork, but using leathered diapasons, fat flutes, ultra-smooth reeds, quintatons, keen strings and octave couplers, he produced an instrument of distorted and warring sonorities completely unrelated to any practical musical purpose. Nowadays no one seriously regards a Hope Jones organ as anything but a freak. But his ideas gained much acceptance in his day and his influence on organ design was utterly deplorable. We have him to thank, too, for the orchestral unit organ, a kind of one-man-band developed under his guidance in the U.S.A. and much used for the accompaniment of silent films.

It took British organ building about fifty years to sink from the classicism of Hill to the eccentricity of Hope Jones; and as long again for a form of classical organ to re-emerge. The intervening period was generally a bleak one. For the most part organ builders were content to perpetuate the end-of-century position with occasional tonal frills and console gadgets. An outstanding exception was the work of Arthur Harrison (of the Durham firm of Harrison and Harrison Ltd) whose sumptuously-constructed and voiced organs at St James, Whitehaven (1904), and Ely Cathedral (1908) preserved something of the classical tradition and set a standard of taste which leading musicians found fully to their liking.

Harrison's outlook was essentially romantic, but he never overlooked the chorus structure an organ must have to be worthy of the name. Thus, in an Harrison organ of any size there were always mixtures on great and swell and a complete family of swell chorus reeds. In this and other things he was guided by Lieutenant-Colonel George Dixon, an influential organ enthusiast of advanced tonal ideas who had known Father Willis, and regarded him as the first British organ builder of importance.

Under Dixon's influence, no doubt, Harrison sought to improve upon Willis by introducing a new element of contrast between great and swell. In a large Willis organ the difference between full great and full swell was purely quantitative, both divisions being capped by reed choruses of identical tone. Harrison 'thickened' the great and 'thinned' the swell. Thus, his great diapason chorus was based on a large, smooth open diapason with leathered lips, and included the complete harmonic series up to twenty-second (the compound stop being a 'harmonics' containing 17th, 19th, flat 21st and 22nd at CC). The great chorus reeds were smooth, opaque trombas on 12 in pressure. Conversely, the swell chorus reeds were thin, refined trumpets (on 8 inches wind); but the swell diapason chorus had a quint mixture and was soft and silvery. It must be confessed that to modern ears a Harrison great diapason chorus with the bright, rather 'edgy' harmonics does not sound very agreeable. But in his very large great organs Harrison provided a second five-rank quint mixture which, since the upperwork was scaled in line with the second diapason, made possible an excellent classical chorus by omitting the large diapason and the harmonics. The main disadvantages of a Harrison are the loudness of the great chorus in relation to

130

the swell and the choir, and the over-weighty pedal organ. In a four-manual organ the choir was an unenclosed miniature great; in a three-manual it was usually an enclosed solo-accompanimental division. The basis of the pedal organ was a large-scale, heavily-blown, open wood bass, and a powerful, smooth ophicleide on up to 20 inches of wind. The strong fundamental of these stops completely eliminated clarity and definition.

Other firms were doing meritorious and even advanced work during the early-twentieth century, in terms of the taste of the day. But Harrison dominated the scene as Willis did the earlier period, and he installed or re-built organs in many cathedrals and important churches.

The Classical Revival

As related earlier, the classical revival movement made no significant impact in Britain until the 1950s. But there were a few inter-war rumblings of discontent among critics and organists. During the 'thirties a few advanced organ builders began to introduce classical features into their tonal schemes. Noteworthy were the solo mutations of the grandson of Father Willis and the above-average provision of upperwork by John Compton in his clever extension organs. The early post-war years saw some tentative though not very successful attempts at classicism, but the movement did not really take root until the opening in 1954 of the organ in the Royal Festival Hall, London.

Most British readers will be familiar with the sound of this organ, which contains a set of classical choruses of a comprehensiveness never before heard in this country. It was designed by the distinguished organist Ralph Downes and executed by Harrison and Harrison under the management of Cuthbert Harrison, the nephew of Arthur Harrison. The organ was much criticized: on grounds of the wastefulness of its tonal design; the incompatibility of the French-voiced chorus reeds with the Anglo-German type of flue-work; and its lack of romantic colours; and generally by persons who were completely out of sympathy with the classical conception of the organ. Yet over a decade later, the instrument has proved itself to be a successful concert organ, by no means lacking in romantic warmth, and able to meet all legitimate musical demands and to convey faithfully the individual styles of the many distinguished organists who have played it.

There is little doubt that the artistic success of the Royal Festival Hall organ helped significantly to change the course of British organ building. By 1960 the British classical revival was an established fact. Many firms, principally Messrs Grant Degens & Bradbeer, Harrison & Harrison, Hill Norman & Beard, N. P. Mander and J. W. Walker & Sons, have all built or re-built organs in the revived idiom. At the time of writing the Wimborne Minister organ, already mentioned, is a recent example. Sometimes the classicism is severe; often, as at Wimborne, there is a fair balance between the classical and the romantic. Except in a few favourable instances it had not been practicable to apply the strict work-disposition; but there has been a marked return to tracker action where conditions allow, with the advantages of modern and more efficient materials. As has been said, the modern tendency in British tonal design is towards the eclectic general-purpose instrument, capable of dealing adequately with all important schools of composition.

The establishment of the classical revival has been accompanied by a wider recognition of the value of our heritage of historic organs. The number of British organs containing unaltered pipework of the eighteenth century or earlier is meagre compared with, say, Holland where there is practically one to every square mile. For all its virtues the Victorian age was one of well-meaning vandalism, when much of the pipework of Smith, Harris, Schrider and others went into the melting pot. That which survives is all the more precious because of its scarcity. Apart from their purely antiquarian interest, such organs are an invaluable source of evidence of past organ-bnilding practice and conditions of performance. Often the effects of age and ill-treatment have clouded the original tone. But since the war, several of these precious instruments have been painstakingly restored to their original freshness. Depending on circumstances, some have been restored 'as new'—as, for instance, the double organ of *c.* 1670 at Adlington Hall near Macclesfield, which is attributed to Father Smith. Other restorations have preserved tracker action and original pipework, but with judicious tonal additions and electric stop and combination action, so that they can cope with music outside the limitations of the original tonal scheme. An example is the Harris-Byfield organ of 1731 at St Vedast, Foster Lane, London. Both these restorations are by N. P. Mander Ltd, the principal exponent of this kind of craftsmanship. A few other firms, notably Hill, Norman & Beard have also done important work in this field.

A moment's reflection on what has been outlined above, together with the reader's personal experience, will show that the present state of the British organ generally is somewhat chaotic. The organist may find himself confronted with any of several different kinds of organ, either in their original or an altered condition. He may, for instance, be required to play an organ which is eighteenth-century in origin, or 'golden age' classic, Victorian romantic, twentieth-century romantic, or classical revival. Registration which sounds good on one kind may sound abysmal on another. The following hints are offered to help him obtain the finest musical results from whatever kind of organ he is called upon to play.

VII

Practical Registration

The Problems Stated

We have now come to the most important part of this book to which all that has been said previously is really by way of introduction: a discussion of the problems of practical registration.

It may seem curious that the greater part of an introductory book on the organ has to be devoted to an explanation of the workings and history of the instrument and only a comparatively small section to its use in music. But the age, complexity and diversity of the organ make this inevitable.

The importance of registration lies in the fact that it is a vital link in the physical chain between composer and listener. If the registration is inappropriate the music is likely to sound wrong, no matter how expert the organist is in the technique of playing the notes. Keyboard technique and registration technique go hand in hand, and skill in one is useless without skill in the other.

It seems to the author that the modern organist, and particularly the beginner organist, is faced with two main problems. The first is to discover whether there are any general rules the observance of which will enable his organ to sound at its best, irrespective of the kind of music which is being played. The second problem is how to use the average British organ in relation to the specific requirements of composers, particularly for the performance of past and foreign schools of organ music for which it is imperfectly suited. The problems of practical registration are conveniently approached under these two headings.

General Principles

The only universal principle is that there are no rigid rules of registration. Registration by rule of thumb will seldom succeed. A set combination which sounds good on one organ will sound bad on another. The musical ear is the only judge, and taste in organ tone, like anything else, can only be acquired by experience. The student should make it his business to hear as many different types of organ as possible, and to assess their tonal possibilities in terms of practical musical use. Hard, objective listening is essential, both at the keys, and at a distance from the instrument. Does this combination sound clear? Does it blend? Does it suit the music and convey the composer's musical ideas in a way that he would approve of? These are the questions that one should continually be asking.

The impracticability of hard and fast rules does not prevent us stating the aims of good registration. They are clarity of texture and the avoidance of aural monotony. All great musical performances in any medium have these two features in common. Dozens of examples could be given: a Toscanini performance of a Brahms symphony, for instance, a Scarlatti sonata played by Landowska on the harpsichord, or Horowitz playing the Liszt Sonata. Every note and outline is clearly defined. Nothing is 'mushy' or blurred. The tone is always sympathetic and the music clear and intelligible.

Organ performances are judged by the same exacting standards, at least by the musical world at large; but how often are they found wanting? Too frequently the texture is confused and the outlines blurred, and the ear longs for relief from the monotony of unrelieved organ tone unimaginatively applied. Sometimes the organ builder is at fault, but the player must take the major share of blame for unmusical results. It is rare that a basically dull and unclear organ cannot be made to sound better with imaginative use. The guiding principles which follow have been proved by experience to be realistically workable, and their intelligent application will improve the effect of any organ performance.

The Effects of Distance

Organ tone is considerably modified by distance. Every effect should be judged from the position of the listener in the body of the building, and adjustment made accordingly. Low pitches carry well, but higher partials are quickly absorbed in the atmosphere. Thus, a combination that sounds top-heavy at the keys may sound perfectly satisfactory in the nave; on the other hand an apparently well-balanced pedal line may sound ponderous and bottom-heavy, and nothing can be more destructive of inner clarity. Distance also reduces the element of contrast. To compensate for this, contrasts between antiphonal choruses, the parts in trios and duos, and solo and accompaniment all need to be intensified at the keys in order to sound convincing to the listener. The balance of power between divisions may also vary according to distance, depending on their location and the way the sound is able to reach the auditorium.

Soft effects that sound well at close quarters will be found to be lost in a large building, and must either be sacrificed or scaled up accordingly.

The effects of distance are most disconcerting in relation to tempo, articulation and phrasing, and it is here particularly that the acoustics of the building must be taken into account. All organ music is reverberant music, and favourable conditions for organ tone require a reverberation period of upwards of two seconds. Reverberation enhances the warmth and carrying power of organ tone; but it also causes smudginess of detail if tempo and articulation are appropriate to acoustically 'dead' conditions. In reverberant conditions tempo needs to be slower and articulation more pronounced if the music is to make sense to the listener at a distance. Much organ playing is too fast. Many organists, even world-famous ones, allow their technique to outstrip their musicianship with the result that no music is created. only a meaningless jumble of sound. The ability to choose the right tempo for a piece in a particular building so that the result is both clear and interesting is one of the hallmarks of an artist.

Sound is absorbed by soft materials such as clothing, and it should not be forgotten that the reverberation period of an empty building will be reduced, perhaps to nothing, when it is full of people. Moreover, the absorption of sound waves will reduce the volume and carrying power of the organ. These factors must all be taken into account in choosing an appropriate registration.

It will be clear, then, that it is essential for the student to listen critically to all his registrations at a distance from the instrument. A friend can be asked to play while he does so. Alternatively the criticism of a musical listener, preferably a non-organist, can be sought. This can often prove instructive. Organists tend to live in a closed world and to be tolerant of their beloved instrument's shortcomings. But if a registration is unacceptable to a non-organist with a good knowledge of orchestral and instrumental music generally, there is likely to be something seriously wrong with it.

Blend

Only stops which blend well should be combined. The careful listener will soon learn to discriminate between stops that are good mixers and those which retain their identity and fight with others in combination. Extreme sonorities such as keen violes, smooth trombas and 'pure' claribel and harmonic flutes are notoriously bad blenders and are best reserved for solo or separate use. The drawstop name is an unreliable guide to the character of the stop and many unsociable sonorities masquerade under innocuous names. On the other hand, stops with 'normal' unforced harmonic development will be found to be good mixers, and practically any reasonable combination of these will yield musical results. The more 'romantic' an organ is, the more likely it is to contain non-blending stops. A characteristic of the classical organ is that it embraces no extreme sonorities and all voices blend without reservation. Provided the blend is pleasing and the result musical there is no reason why any combination of stops should not be used. The only test is whether it is apposite to the music under performance.

There is a currently held view that flutes should never be mixed with open diapasons. This is quite mistaken and dates from the romantic pre-1940 period when flutes were often very 'oily' and diapasons hard and stringy. Every combination must be judged on its merits. A stringy Schulze type of diapason and a harmonic flute 4 ft will no more blend than oil and water. Indeed, almost any kind of open diapason will be spoiled by the cloying tone of a harmonic flute. But 'normal' flutes—Gedeckt, Quintade, stopped diapason, Rohrflöte, Spitzflöte, even some unpretentious open cylindrical flutes—will blend admirably with 'normal' diapason tone and the result will be a new kind of tone colour. Flutes of this kind are intended to be used in chorus where extra fullness is needed. We have already seen that the stopped diapason was considered to play an important part in the old English full great. And in baroque organs, tonal pyramids of principal stops were often erected on a neutral flute foundation as we have seen. The important point is not to draw all the 8 ft and 4 ft flue stops in 'full' effects as a matter of course, but to use them selectively in accordance with the 'economy of choice' principle explained below.

Economy of Choice

It is sound general practice never to use more stops than are necessary to yield a desired effect. The result will nearly always be an improvement in clarity, steadiness and purity of tone. Limit the chorus combinations to essential structural stops and select only one of each pitch unless there is good reason to do otherwise. It is instructive to hold a chord on a full great and gradually put in stops, observing how many are not really needed. Many inessential stops are inaudible in chorus. Others are heard but impair the purity of effect. Whether they are heard or not they may swallow wind which would enable the structural stops to sound louder and steadier. They may also cause unpleasantness by being slightly out of tune since, with varying temperatures, no organ will stay finely tuned throughout for long.

Thus, a great diapason chorus will always gain in transparency

IX. Organ at the Jacobikirche, Lübeck, 1504–1673. Another drawing
from Dr A. G. Hill's great work illustrating the 'work principle'
arrangement of great organ, back-positive organ and pedal organ
disposed in two side towers.

if only one open diapason is used and the flutes are omitted. This does not mean that a second open diapason and the flutes must never be used in full chorus, but that they should only be used where extra fullness is desired, not as a matter of course. When a great clarion 4 ft is sounding the principal 4 ft can often be withdrawn without loss. When the great reeds are brought on at the end of a gradual build-up, the swell reed chorus, except perhaps the 16 ft, can often be dispensed with, so that there is less chance of the out-of-tuneness to which reed stops are particularly subject.

The same reasoning applies to all chorus divisions. There is no point in drawing the soft pedal basses in full combinations. They will not be heard and are greedy wind-consumers. The full swell effect will benefit by reduction to the essential reed chorus and flue upperwork above 4 ft.

Tonal Variety and Aural Relief

Because of its sustained, unyielding nature organ tone palls more quickly than the tone of more expressive instruments. This makes it necessary to ensure the utmost tonal variety during performance. The problem of how to achieve tonal variety is not solved by making kaleidoscopic and musically irrelevant changes of registration during a particular composition. Unless related to the musical structure, changes of registration are irritating to a sensitive listener; and many compositions, J. S. Bach's particularly, need straightforward registration schemes with minimal stop changes.

The solution is to be found rather in good programme planning and in selecting the stops so as to get plenty of musically relevant tonal variety during an entire recital or church service. Few organists exploit the tonal possibilities of their instruments as effectively as they could. There are several ways in which this can be done.

An organ with a reasonably complete tonal scheme will normally be able to produce several different kinds of *piano, mezzoforte* or *fortissimo*. Consider the Wimborne great organ, for example (p. 48). One loud combination might consist of open diapason no. 2, principal, fifteenth and mixture. This will be thin, bright and clear. Another combination, full and reedier, but less brilliant, consists of quintade, both open diapasons, principal, twelfth, fifteenth and tierce. The difference is probably not great in terms of decibels, but it is considerable in terms of contrast and relief. These are two obvious examples; a little thought and experimentation will show that the possibilities are extensive.

With smaller schemes the possibilities are clearly more limited, but they are still exploitable. Consider the following six-stop great organ:

Open diapason	8
Stopped diapason	8
Principal	4
Chimney flute	4
Twelfth	$2\frac{2}{3}$
Fifteenth	2

This contains at least four distinct loud effects each involving three stops:

Open diapason, principal and fifteenth
Stopped diapason, principal and fifteenth
Open diapason, flute and fifteenth
Stopped diapason, flute and fifteenth

The addition of the twelfth to these effects increases the total to eight apart from the full great proper. When coupling to other divisions is taken into account the possibilities are considerable, and the imaginative student will have no difficulty in working out what they are.

Tonal variety at the *mezzoforte* and *piano* level can be greatly increased by using single 8 ft stops. Quiet flutes, strings and reeds which sound boring and non-blending in combination are often refreshing when used separately. It should not be forgotten that adding one 8 ft stop to another is comparatively ineffective, but that the addition of stops at octave or super-octave pitch results in a distinct tonal change. Adding an 8 ft open flute to an 8 ft Gedeckt sounds uninteresting even if it is noticeable. But combining two such stops at 8 ft and 4 ft pitch produces a new and interesting tone-colour. Much variety can be obtained by 'crossing' related 8 ft and 4 ft stops. For example, a swell organ often includes:

Open diapason	8
Lieblich Gedeckt	8
Principal	4
Stopped flute	4

The 'family' combinations are diapason and principal, Lieblich Gedeckt and flute. The 'crossed' combinations for increased variety are Lieblich Gedeckt and principal, diapason and flute. The possibilities are greater when doubles and 2 ft stops are taken into account, and here again, the student can apply his imagination to the problem.

The use of doubles an octave higher, singly or combined with higher pitched stops, is another useful means of extending the tonal resources of an organ, provided the compass of the music permits it. For example, where there are no mutation stops above 2 ft, the combination of great bourdon 16 ft, flute 8 ft and twelfth, transposed up an octave and sounding as 8 ft, 4 ft and 1⅓ ft, may provide a pleasing larigot effect otherwise unobtainable.

The possibilities of tonal contrast are reduced, and consequently the risk of aural fatigue increased, by too much use of coupled manuals. In music such as a Howells psalm prelude, or service settings of the 'Noble in B minor' kind, it is necessary to couple the swell to the great both to bridge the gaps in the great build-up and to provide an expressive accompaniment to the rise and fall of the voices. But if great and swell are always coupled, they lose their individuality and there is no longer the possibility of contrasting combinations on the two divisions. Coupling manuals together limits resources by merging two or more divisions into one. It is far better to keep them separate as a general rule and to couple only when the combined effect is musically expedient.

The effectiveness of any tonal colour diminishes in proportion to its frequency of use. This applies particularly to exciting effects such as the full swell and brilliant solo reeds. These are thrilling in small doses, but soon become wearisome if overdone. For the same reason it is wise to ration the use of manual and pedal doubles and exotic soft effects such as the voix céleste, vox humana, and combinations involving the tremulant. The modern fashion for 'baroque' registration has led many organists to overdo the effect of flute 8 ft and fifteenth 2 ft. Such effects are clear and pleasing in the right context, but they soon pall and much harm is done to the cause of classical registration if they are not used with caution and taste. Often a fifteenth is too biting to sound well in any such combination.

Loudness

Loud effects and increases in loudness need to be carefully controlled. The perception of loudness is a highly subjective matter. A rough law, known as the Weber-Fechner law of sensation, states that an increase of energy in a source of sound, light, weight, and so on, which can just be perceived as an increase of sensation, always bears the same ratio to the unaugmented source of energy. In terms of registration this means that the louder one is playing at any particular time the greater is the amount of tone that must be added to enable increased loudness to be comfortably noticeable. Slight additions of tone after a period of quiet playing are consequently more telling than considerable additions after *mezzoforte* or *forte* playing. Moreover, much organ playing is far too loud. The apparent loudness of a combination is conditioned by the level to which the ear has become accustomed. It is a mistake, therefore, to begin a recital with a lengthy loud piece. The ear soon regards the level of volume as the norm and the organist is left with fewer resources for climactic effects or tonal variety. A brilliant and loud opening piece is certainly initially effective. But a few pieces calling for subdued and varied tones will more effectively pave the way for a piece displaying the louder combinations and choruses. Long periods of practice will be less tiring (and consequently more beneficial) if clear *mezzoforte* combinations are used rather than full choruses, reeds and upperwork.

The full power of a large organ soon loses its significance if used at the end of every piece. But it can be electrifying if saved up for the climax of a big central piece or for the end of a recital. It is worth while observing in the concert hall how a great conductor will keep the full strength of the orchestra in reserve.

Variety of Build-up

Many compositions do not require a gradual increase or decrease in tone. But for those that do, a smoother build-up will be achieved if the Weber-Fechner ratio is kept in mind and stops are added in the order that produces a just perceptible increase in loudness. This must be decided empirically according to the peculiarities of the organ in use. Tonal variety can be increased by varying the order of build-up. For example, the twelfth can occasionally be added before the fifteenth, or the large open diapason and double diapason can be added after the mixtures are sounding. A complete set of chorus reeds can be added in the order 16 ft, 4 ft, 8 ft, or 4 ft, 16 ft, 8 ft, rather than in the conventional order 8 ft, 4 ft, 16 ft. Any tonal increase which can be obtained by adding non-unison stops (that is, stops of pitches other than 8 ft) will be more colourful, interesting and less aurally tiring than one obtained by adding stops of 8 ft pitch.

Chorus Proportion

The internal balance of chorus effects—the power relationship between individual chorus ranks—is germane to the avoidance of tonal tedium. It is a fact of practical experience that a musical sound in which the acoustic energy is spread over a wide field is less fatiguing than one in which it is narrowly concentrated. This has already been touched upon in our explanation of mixtures and upperwork on page 39.

In a classical diapason chorus the acoustic energy is spread more or less equally over several gently-voiced ranks in which no particular pitch predominates. The effect is of power without loudness. It palls less quickly than, say, a concentration of 16 ft, 8 ft and 4 ft stops of similar output. This is why the *organo pleno* of the organ at St Laurens Alkmaar, for example, is so apt a medium for large-scale Bach organ works. It is aurally interesting for at least the eight-to-ten-minute duration of a long prelude and fugue.

It is a good policy, therefore, to spread the energy of chorus effects as widely as possible by selecting ranks of similar output but different pitch, and by excluding any pitch which seems to be unduly emphasized. In many great organs possessing large and small unison diapasons, the chorus builds up satisfactorily on the small diapason, or perhaps on a flute. But when the large open diapason is drawn the upperwork seems suspended in mid-air and completely unrelated to the foundation tone. Similarly, in the full swell the 8 ft trumpet or cornopean is often a thickening ingredient which is better omitted. A better full swell often consists of reeds 16 ft and 4 ft together with mixture and octave coupler—because the energy is widely and evenly spread.

Adding a loud 8 ft of any kind to a well-proportioned chorus can be relied upon to destroy all its proportions and musical character. This applies particularly to tubas and other loud reeds. Except in very large buildings, such stops are intended exclusively for solo use. Used in single notes against a full chorus accompaniment, or antiphonally, they may be impressive and musically relevant. But to couple a tuba to a balanced set of fluc and reed choruses is the height of unmusical vulgarity. What artistic conductor would allow the strings and woodwind to be annihilated by the brass?

To add octave and sub-octave couplers to a well-proportioned chorus is a sure way of spoiling it. Except in the rare instances where an extra octave of treble pipes is provided, it should not be forgotten that these couplers reduce the manual compass by an octave at each end. They should therefore be used with special discretion. A sensible use of octave couplers is for augmenting soft effects, and covering up the deficiencies of a tonal design. For instance, on a small organ a big full swell effect can sometimes be faked by drawing an 8 ft reed, mixture and octave couplers. Similarly, an inadequate swell or choir chorus can on occasion be brightened by the octave coupler to serve as a tolerable substitute for a properly developed positive organ. But whether expedients of this kind work satisfactorily depends on circumstances. It is obviously inartistic to use octave couplers if the result is a screech at one end and a growl at the other.

In much French music written for the Cavaillé-Coll organ the manual writing lies high in the compass, and a grand orgue sub-octave coupler was provided for filling in loud passages. In British organs it is desirable, and sometimes essential, to use the swell sub-octave, or swell sub-octave to great coupler for this purpose.

Solo and Accompaniment

Solo and accompaniment need to be clearly distinguishable. Solo colours are ineffective if the accompaniment has the same kind of harmonic make-up. An open diapason or oboe, for example, should never be accompanied by a salicional or dulciana; nor a stopped diapason by a Lieblich Gedeckt. But a Spitzflöte or even a colourful Rohrflöte might be expected to sound well against a stopped diapason, the harmonic composition being different. In a smallish building the contrasts need not be great; but in a large one they will need to be intensified owing to the effects of distance. A highly colourful solo effect will sound more intense against a neutral flute background. However, care should be taken to ensure that the accompaniment is not too soft to be heard: it is just as important musically as the solo part.

It is not necessary to rely upon exclusively solo stops and mutations for solo effects. Ordinary flutes, open diapasons and chorus reeds make excellent solo stops on occasion.

A little more must be said about the use of flute mutations for synthetic tone-building, the technique of which has already been outlined in other parts of this book. Almost any permutation of nazard, tierce, larigot and 8 ft, 4 ft or 2 ft flutes will produce

Practical Registration

acceptable results. The mutations can be superimposed on a flute or string foundation; in each case the result will be found to be different and interesting. The only rule is that the tierce should *never* be used without the nazard if a disagreeable tone is to be avoided. If the solo extends below middle C or thereabouts it is generally advisable to include a 4 ft flute; otherwise the gap between the 8 ft and higher pitches may be too noticeable. The tone of solo reeds such as the oboe, clarinet or vox humana can be effectively intensified by adding mutations or 4 ft and 2 ft flutes—provided the reed is in tune!

Use of the Swell Box

Swell effects are required by many composers and are undeniably effective when intelligently applied. But to use the swell box to best advantage it is necessary to recognize its limitations.

The swell box is perhaps the most 'unnatural' of all organ effects. It is an attempt to make static organ tone seem to yield a kind of expression which is contrary to its essential nature. The dynamic crescendo of orchestral instruments is produced by an increase and intensification of harmonics: by a qualitative change as well as an increase of loudness. The crescendo of the swell is simulated by the rather crude device of letting out more sound, and the effect is quite different. The change is mainly quantitative except that the closed shutters dampen the fundamental of the tone. Everyone knows the sound of a good orchestral crescendo. But suppose the orchestra were shut in a chamber and instructed to play *fortissimo* throughout, while the conductor applied 'expression' by opening and shutting doors. Absurd, certainly; but this, without too much exaggeration, is what happens in the organ swell. And it is a reason why many people find its effects artificial and irritating.

It is unwise, therefore, to regard the swell as a substitute for the true dynamic crescendo obtained by adding stops in chorus order; or to accentuate its artificiality by using it unnaturally. For example, it is pointless to start a solo almost inaudibly and gradually increase the volume. Orchestral instruments do not behave in this way. Nor is the end of an orchestral solo normally faded out to nothingness. To use the swell box in this way nearly always sounds wrong and with some stops, can seem to produce a disturbing flattening of pitch.

As with all organ effects, the impact of the swell is increased by restrained use. Also, its use needs to be related to a musical context for it to be purposeful—rather than just something to do when a foot happens to be freed from pedalling. The Weber-Fechner law explains why the first few millimetres of box opening are more dynamic than the later stages. With a good swell box it is better to open the early stages gradually and to take care not to open too much too soon.

The simulated crescendo is by no means the only, or indeed the most important, function of the swell. It can be used to adjust the static levels of volume between divisions or between solo and accompaniment; to quieten a manual into an echo division; or to mingle one tone-colour with another.

If a smooth but natural dynamic build-up is needed it is best to combine both swell box and the stop addition methods of crescendo. Couple the swell to the great and add stops in chorus order, gradually opening the box so as to bridge the gaps between the additions.

Use of the Extension Organ

Registration on organs constructed on the extension or unit system needs to be chosen with especial care in order to avoid the two main pit-falls of such instruments: missing notes and the colourlessness of effects obtained by mere octave coupling. A little experimentation will soon reveal which stops have parent ranks in common, despite the different names on the stop labels. The solution then is simple: avoid, so far as possible, selecting adjacent pitches drawn from the same rank. For example, on the extension organ specified on page 66 the combinations:

Spitzflöte 8 ft, 4 ft and 2 ft,
stopped diapason 8 ft, 4 ft and 2 ft

will be found to lack colour because they are obtained by octave couplings of the same sonority; and because of the adjacent octave couplings the risk of missing notes will be great. But if the stops are selected thus:

Spitzflöte	8 ft	2 ft
Stopped diapason	4 ft	

or:

Spitzflöte	4 ft	
Stopped diapason 8 ft		2 ft

the result will be virtually indistinguishable from a straight organ. These are two obvious examples. The more any extension organ is used on these lines, the better it will sound.

The Tremulant

Not very long ago it was the fashion to despise the tremulant as a fancy effect unworthy of the dignity of the organ. With the establishment of the classical revival, however, the value of this ancient and, when tastefully used, most beautiful organ effect is once again appreciated. J. S. Bach's insistence that the tremulant at St Blasiuskirche, Mühlhausen, should be properly regulated is well known. Nowadays it is by no means uncommon to hear a tremulant inducing a gentle waving effect into the coloratura melody of a Bach chorale prelude, and this is undoubtedly one of its legitimate uses. It is important that the best of the tremulant should be neither too violent nor too fast. Many tremulants flutter unpleasantly. A gentle beat of about $2\frac{1}{2}$ to a second seems ideal. Where there is no céleste stop, a good tremulant used with a dulciana or soft string stop is an effective substitute.

By registering in accordance with the principles outlined above the general effect of any organ will gain in clarity and tonal contrast. But any organ effect, no matter how intrinsically interesting it may be, is pointless unless used in an appropriate musical context. This brings us to the second problem—registration in relation to styles of organ music and the requirements of composers.

Making the Best of the Average British Organ

There is much old organ music for which the average British organ is to a greater or lesser degree unsuitable. By the 'average British organ' is meant any romantic or semi-classical organ built in Britain during about the past 100 years—the kind of organ the student or ordinary organist is most likely to encounter. The music with which we are mainly concerned falls into four groups:

(i)   German: seventeenth and eighteenth century
(ii) French: seventeenth and eighteenth century
(iii) Italian: sixteenth to eighteenth century
(iv) British: sixteenth to early nineteenth century.

Something must also be said about the registration of nineteenth-century and modern music generally, though not much since it represents a more widely understood idiom.

We will consider the old music first. If the organist is fortunate enough to have the use of a new or rebuilt classical instrument, the authentic registration of any of the four groups will present few problems. It is only necessary to take into account the resources available to the composer and the style of his music, since a good modern classical organ is capable of coping with all schools and church service accompaniment. On an historic British organ much of the old music, especially the French school, can be performed with reasonable authenticity; though the inadequacy of the old pedal divisions and the lack of solo mutations will present some difficulties. Unfortunately both historic, and at the present time classical, organs are few in number compared with 'average British organs'.

Any musician with a sense of historical period and style will find the performance of old music in a fundamentally unsuitable medium repugnant. The ideal solution—only to perform music for which an organ is properly adapted—is quite impractical, certainly for the student. The latter will want to master the instrument, and to learn as wide a selection of the repertoire as possible (in which the works of J. S. Bach will inevitably

149

predominate). He will want to learn to perform this music to the finest possible effect, and in so doing he will have to come to terms with the average British organ.

There cannot be many leading recitalists and teachers nowadays who would not agree that the music we are now considering cannot adequately be performed on the average British organ without a great deal of 'faked' registration, that is, using the resources of the organ unconventionally and in a manner not envisaged by its designers. We will now consider some of the ways in which this can be done.

In relation to the performance of the German school the deficiencies of the average British organ are four-fold:

(i) The lack of a primary flue chorus of sufficient vitality and transparency
(ii) The lack of a secondary (positive) flue chorus of contrasted tone but equal volume
(iii) The lack of an independent pedal organ of well defined tone quality; and
(iv) The lack of appropriate solo effects, particularly those obtained by means of flute mutations.

The older the organ the less likely it will be that these faults will be apparent.

In many organs built between roughly 1850 and 1900 (by Hill, Walker, Willis, Gray & Davison, Holdich, and some lesser-known makers) the great diapason chorus builds up on classical lines in ranks of similar volume. By continental standards the number of mixture ranks will be inadequate; but the general effect is clear and lively, and a more than tolerable substitute for the *organo pleno* effect. The later the organ, the more likely is the main open diapason to predominate in chorus; if it does, a second open diapason or a flute can be substituted for it with improved effect. This will almost certainly be necessary in the case of organs made between about 1900 and 1950, since the major diapason will be too loud to fulfil any satisfactory chorus function. A difficulty is that the chorus may then sound unpleasantly thin. If so, it must be filled out by

150

drawing the flutes. The result may not be ideal, but it will be the best that can be achieved in the circumstances.

Discretion should be exercised in the choice of mixtures. If the only great mixture contains a strong tierce, it is best omitted in lengthy movements, or perhaps saved up until final return to the great after an episode on another manual. It may be possible to rectify the lack of a great mixture by coupling the swell one—perhaps with the swell octave coupler if the result is not too thin or top-heavy. If the only compound stop is an harmonics, there will be no choice but to leave it out, since the effect will inevitably be displeasing. Father Willis's tierce mixtures are normally unobjectionable.

The difficulty of obtaining a secondary flue chorus loud enough to be used against a full-blooded great to mixture may be insuperable. The earlier swell flue choruses of Hill, Walker, and Gray & Davison are often bright enough to form a tolerable Rückpositiv or Oberwerk substitute. Even some late nineteenth-century swells, Walker's particularly, are quite bold. But the worst offender was Willis, whose swell diapason choruses were too restrained and whose example was followed by Harrison and others. Where this is so, the swell can sometimes be boosted by coupling to the choir; but this cannot be done where the action is original tracker, or pneumatic lever and there is no swell to choir coupler. Moreover, if the choir is an enclosed semi-solo division, its contribution will anyway be ineffective. There are then only two expedients. The swell can be brightened by octave coupling or perhaps by adding the clarion. If this is unsatisfactory, as it may well be, the only alternative is to reduce the great so as to secure a reasonable balance between the two divisions. The lesser of the two evils must be chosen according to circumstances.

The difficulty of obtaining satisfactory inter-manual balances on the average British organ makes it all the more necessary to ask oneself a question relevant to the performance of baroque organ music generally: even on an ideal instrument, are manual changes called for by the structure of a particular composition? In relation to the performance of Bach at least, many musicologists believe that manual changes in certain movements were never intended. There is good reason to believe, for instance, that the B minor prelude (BWV 544) was intended to be played *organo pleno* throughout with no Rückpositiv episodes. The subject is too complex to be argued here, but Walter Emery has stated a convincing case in an article in the *Musical Times,* and the reader is urged to look it up.*

In using the average pedal organ the main problem is to keep the bass independent of the tenor and prevent it dominating all else. This is best solved by coupling, as far as possible, to some manual other than the main one in use (e.g., to the swell and/or the choir when playing on the great) and by controlling carefully the quantity of 16 ft pedal tone. Mid-nineteenth-century pedal open wood basses were fairly soft and prompt-speaking. These and many a free-toned *mezzoforte* 16 ft trombone of the same period can provide an appropriate well-defined 16 ft pedal line in an *organo pleno*. Since their bloated twentieth-century counterparts have none of these virtues, there is no choice but to leave them out of the picture. In most late nineteenth- and twentieth-century organs (particularly where the great must be coupled to the pedals), anything more than bourdons 16 ft and 8 ft may be too loud, unless a violone or an open metal 16 ft borrowed from the great is available. Medium-volume reed tone in 16 ft, 8 ft and 4 ft pitches is a satisfactory means of achieving pedal definition. When the swell 16 ft reed is borrowed on the pedals in 16 ft or higher pitches, this is all to the good; otherwise one can only make the swell reeds available by the inconvenience of coupling.

The lack of appropriate solo reed and mutation effects is best considered in relation to the French school, since they are more essential for its proper performance than for the German. Again, the older the organ, the more adaptable it will be. In nineteenth-century organs the twelfth often tends towards flutiness, or is soft, and can be used convincingly with the 8 ft and 4 ft flutes as a solo nasard. Many sesquialteras break to

* *Musical Times,* June and July 1962, 'On the Registration of Bach's Organ Preludes and Fugues'.

12th, 15th, 17th at middle C and can be combined with 8 ft and 4 ft stops to compound a cornet. The difficulty is how to fake the *tierce en taille*. The normal sesquialtera cannot be used because of the breaks below middle C (one should never use a breaking mixture in solo where the breaks cut across the melodic line), and there is no choice but to make do with the nasard effect, or perhaps to add some reediness by coupling a clarinet.

Nineteenth-century low-pressure reeds usually have sufficient attack and character to serve for the more dramatic French versions. Nearly all old stops labelled 'cremona' or 'clarionet' have much of the vitality of an eighteenth-century cromorne. Old light-pressure trumpets attack well enough in the bass to do duty as a *basse de trompette*. Any defect of attack, regularity or intensity can be covered up by the traditional method of adding flue stops, 4 ft and 2 ft, or even a mixture. Father Willis's light-pressure reeds, however, will be fine enough to stand without flue support. His full-blooded corno di bassetto stops are highly effective in music scored for cromorne.

Although the *grand jeu* is not a solo effect, it may be considered here. Again, old light-pressure reeds will serve best, and their weak trebles and irregularities can be disguised by drawing diapason upperwork. But there is no need to include flue stops on ideological grounds alone. When, as in a Father Willis organ, reeds are regular and the trebles well kept up, they are best heard alone.

In an organ of the 1900–1950 period the probability is that the diapason twelfth will be far too loud and bright to serve as a nasard. The great mixture, particularly if it is an harmonics, will be unpleasant in solo use. The chorus reeds may be too loud, or deficient in attack, or both. The choir clarinet will almost certainly be far too genteel to be convincing in cromorne solos, though the addition of flue stops may improve it. Perhaps the best use of the clarinet in old music is with a 2 ft piccolo added as a voix humaine substitute. For the most part the feeble flute and dulciana mutations that appeared in choir organs during the 1920s and 1930s are an inadequate substitute for the strong French solo mutations. They were, however, a step in the right direction, and are often better than nothing. It is difficult to escape the conclusion that the average 1900–1950 organ is little use for old French and German music demanding dramatic solo colours, and that little can be done about it.

The needs of the Italian and the pre-Restoration British schools have enough in common to be considered together.

The canzoni of Frescobaldi or the organ fantasias of Orlando Gibbons, to take only two examples, are best expressed through the unspectacular medium of gentle-toned 8 ft, 4 ft and 2 ft flutes or diapasons. Historical precedent allows the addition of a well-balanced quint mixture in the louder Italian pieces (the *organo pieno*) but powerful flue stops and reeds of any kind are quite inappropriate. To purist ears the use of 16 ft pedal tone in this kind of music will sound incongruous. English organs of the period had no pedals, and the Italian only pedal pull-downs sounding at the manual pitch. In registering British double organ voluntaries it is worth remembering that the basic pitch of the chair organ was an octave higher than the great. Thus, it would be appropriate to select, say, swell Gedeckt 8 ft, and principal 4 ft for the 'single' organ, and great small open diapason and stopped diapason (or flute) 8 ft and principal 4 ft for the 'double'. For the Italian piffaro (used in pieces such as the *Toccata per l'Elevazione* of Frescobaldi), a dulciana or salicional voix celéste, box open, may be expected to provide the right degree of colourful restfulness. Better still, the celéstes, if not too stringy, may sound well with a soft open diapason.

The problems posed by the British school of 1660 to *c.* 1840 (Purcell and Blow to early S. S. Wesley) are much the same as those of the French school. The British school demands neither *grand jeu,* nor solo mutation effects except the cornet and sesquialtera. Otherwise the solo demands are similar and the same solutions apply.

In selecting a suitable British 'full organ' or, for that matter, a French *plein jeu,* the same considerations apply as in choosing a German *organo pleno. Mezzoforte* 8 ft and 4 ft chorus reeds can be included in the 'full organ' effect, however, and a strong

X. Interior of the organ at Christ Church, Bermuda (N. P. Mander Ltd, 1967), showing the great organ soundboard. The traditional arrangement of pipes in two sides is shown: the right-hand 'C' side (CC, DD, EE, FF sharp, GG sharp, AA sharp, etc) and the left-hand 'C sharp' side (CC sharp, DD sharp, FF, GG, AA, BB, etc). Its purpose is to distribute the weight symmetrically over the soundboard area. From right to left the stops are:

(1) mixture 111 ranks (5) nason flute 4 ft
(2) fifteenth 2 ft   (6) dulciana 8 ft, and
(3) twelfth 2 2/3 ft   (7) stopped diapason metal 8 ft
(4) principal 4 ft

The large pipes in the left of the picture are part of the open diapason 8 ft bass. Most of the pipes of this stop stand in the front of the organ case (to the left of the picture, partly hidden) and receive their wind through metal tubing connected to the corresponding soundboard holes.

tierce mixture is not out of character, nor objectionable in the short movements where this effect is indicated.

The transcription for the modern organ compass of music written for the transitional British organ 1800–1840 (with FFF or GGG manuals and pull-down pedals) presents some difficulties. Certain compositions by William Russell and the Wesleys contain passages which run below the manual and pedal compasses of the modern organ. Such music must therefore be transcribed; but the musical result will suffer if this is done inartistically. A detailed discussion of this problem is beyond the scope of this book. However, two points are put forward for thought. Firstly, when an obbligato pedal part is scored, it is intended to be heard at the manual (pull-down) pitch of 8 ft. So, an appropriate effect may be obtained by playing on uncoupled 16 ft pedal stops an octave higher—the solution suggested by S. S. Wesley. The second point is purely the personal view of the author. The student is recommended, whenever possible, to obtain the music in an original-text edition (of which there are plenty available) and to make his own performing edition, taking care to play the original notes at the pitch at which they were meant to be heard.

In the author's opinion, this is to be preferred to using an unscholarly performing edition where an editor has transferred the bass wholesale to the pedals and added inner parts to give the left hand something to do.

As mentioned above, nineteenth-century and modern organ music can be dealt with briefly. Some composers, such as Mendelssohn, Reubke, Liszt, Brahms, Rheinberger, Reger and Hindemith were primarily interested in dynamic changes. Others, such as Franck (and the French symphonic school generally) and in our own day, Messiaen, Langlais, and Flor Peters are 'colourists' and call for particular sonorities as well as dynamics.

In performing the primarily 'dynamic' composers, it is only possible to deploy the resources of an organ in the way which seems best to follow their dynamic markings and bring out the musical meaning. Nineteenth-century German organs, though 'romantic' compared with those they superseded, were none the less more classically designed (and consequently more tonally transparent) than most of our twentieth-century ones. These tend to give the thickly-scored music of Reger, for instance, a turgidity it was never meant to possess. For this reason, German romantic music invariably sounds better if it is registered as transparently as possible in accordance with the hints given above. The lack of a general stop-crescendo device is a disadvantage in playing music calling for 'Rollschweller' dynamics. Given a plentiful supply of adjustable pistons, it is often difficult to add and take off the stops gradually and smoothly, and it is worth while employing an assistant to act as a human Rollschweller.

Turning to the 'colourists', the diversity among organs clearly makes it impossible to interpret many of their instructions literally. One can again only try to realize a composer's requirements as faithfully as possible within available resources. The greatest problem arises in dealing with the French symphonic school whose music is registered fairly precisely in terms of the Cavaillé-Coll organ. Literal transference of these instructions to the average British organ would be absurd because of its different tonal design and system of control. The standard French instruction *tous les claviers acouplis* applies only to the ventil system. It must be resolutely ignored, and appropriate blocks of foundation, or reed and mixture, tone should be added or withdrawn under the British system in accordance with the composer's directions.

The direction *fonds de 8 pied,* meaning the singing composite foundation tone of the French organ, will not be met on the average British organ by drawing all the 8 ft stops. A small open diapason, perhaps with a well-blending flute, may be nearer the desired effect. No one doubts that Franck, in specifying trompette solos in his *Prière* and E major and A minor Chorals had in mind the delicate récit trompette at Ste Clotilde. This is far removed from the average swell cornopean. Unless a non-strident low-pressure trumpet is available, the hautboy will be more appropriate for this introspective music. Again, Franck often asks for *fonds de 8 pied et hautbois.* This is all very well on a

Cavaillé-Coll in the sympathetic acoustics of Ste Clotilde, but on the average British organ it is likely to be far from felicitous. Some more sympathetic, though necessarily reedy, combination must be sought.

If a moral emerges from all that has been said above, it is that the basic approach to British organ registration should be pragmatic. The best registration for a particular composition must be decided in the light of conditions and resources: the character of the instrument, its position, the acoustics and size of the building, the style of the music and what is known of the composer's wishes. All this calls for historical knowledge, a sensitive ear, taste, and a wide experience of different organs.

The painstaking organist will approach an unfamiliar instrument with a completely open mind. He will try all the stops, observing their character, their balance between treble and bass, and their blending power and proportion in chorus, and the balance of power between the different divisions, both from a distance and at the keys. He will note the type of action and its response in relation to the speech-initiation of the pipes. Having in this way assessed the musical capabilities of the organ, he will choose his programme so as to do the best for the music and for the organ, and set about performing it as clearly and intelligibly as he can. If this is done, the mutual enjoyment of performer and audience will be increased, and something more will have been done to convince the musical world at large that the organ is after all a fine and noble musical instrument, and that some of the world's greatest composers were not wrong to entrust their profoundest thoughts to its players.

PART III

SELECT GLOSSARY OF ORGAN STOPS

Select Glossary of Organ Stops*

Acoustic bass, Harmonic bass, Resultant A pedal flue stop in which a resultant 32 ft pitch is generated cheaply but in-effectively by coupling a 16 ft stop with the fifth above; e.g., open diapason 16 ft and bourdon 10⅔ ft, or bourdon 16 ft and quint 10⅔ ft taken from the same rank

Acuta (Italian, 'sharp'; German: Scharf) A high-pitched mixture

Aeoline A soft, delicate 8 ft string stop

Apfelregal (German, 'appleregal') An old reed stop of *Regal*† type (q.v.), with apple-shaped resonators

Baarpijp (Dutch) A flue stop of *Gemshorn* type (q.v.) in Dutch organs

Bachflöte (German) A *Gemshorn* (q.v.)

Bärpfeife (German) A gruff-sounding *Regal* (q.v.)

Baryton A 16 ft *Vox humana* (q.v.)

Bass A prefix indicating that a manual stop is of double (16 ft) pitch, e.g., bass clarinet 16 ft, bass tuba 16 ft

Basset-horn See *Corno di bassetto*

---

* Since the origin of many stop names is complex and obscure, only straight-forward derivations are given. For fuller information the reader is referred to the Glossary in P. L. Williams' *The European Organ* (London, 1966).

† When stops appear in italics, the reader is referred to a separate entry.

Select Glossary of Organ Stops

Bassflute An 8 ft pedal flute, often an extension of the *Bourdon* 16 ft (q.v.)

Bassoon (Italian: fagotto; French: basson; German: Fagott) A small-scale reed with conical tubes voiced with a likeness to the tone of the orchestral instrument. A favourite and effective 16 ft chorus reed in British swell organs under the common name of contra fagotto. On solo and choir organs, however, a bassoon is usually a 16 ft version, sometimes an extension, of the 8 ft orchestral oboe (see *Hautboy*)

Bazuin A pedal reed of trumpet-like quality, 32 ft or 16 ft pitch, found in Dutch organs

Blockflöte (German, 'recorder': sometimes half-anglicized as 'blockflute') See *Recorder*

Bombarde (i) A manual division containing a powerful reed chorus and diapason upperwork.
(ii) A trumpet-type chorus reed, normally of 16 ft pitch on manuals or pedals. It is usually found in French, or French-influenced organs

Bombardon A pedal reed of 32 ft or 16 ft pitch with a tone quality something between a *Bombarde* and a *Bassoon* (q.v.)

Bourdon (French: bourdonner, 'to buzz'; German: Bordun; Italian: bordone) A stopped flute. Usually a 16 ft pedal stop of wooden pipes (sometimes called 'subbass'); also a quiet manual double sometimes duplexed on the pedals. In small British organs it is usually the only pedal 16 ft stop, and often extended to provide a bassflute 8 ft and higher pitches. 32 ft bourdons appear on the pedals and on large great organs. Manual bourdons of smaller scale than normal are called 'lieblich bourdons'. Metal bourdons of 8 ft pitch frequently appear on the manuals of French organs. They are the counterpart of the German *Gedeckt* and the British *Stopped diapason,* but are sometimes of chimney flute or *Rohrflöte* construction (q.v.)

Carillon (i) A compound stop containing octave, fifth and third-sounding ranks designed to suggest the sound of small bells.

162

(ii) A percussion stop consisting of tubular bells struck by hammers and worked by pneumatic or electric action

Céleste (French, 'heavenly') See *Voix céleste*

Celestina A soft, small-scale open wood flute of 4 ft pitch; invented by William Hill

Cello See *Violoncello*

Chalumeau (French; German: Schalmai; English: shawm) A reed stop voiced in imitation of the old musical instrument, a forerunner of the clarinet. It has half-length, narrow, cylindrical tubes and a bright, somewhat nasal tone. In modern British organs it is usually a pedal solo reed of 4 ft or 2 ft. pitch. See also *Rohr Schalmai*

Chimney flute See *Rohrflöte*

Choral bass A 4 ft pedal stop of principal tone, so-called because it is required to sustain the 4 ft *cantus firmus* in certain chorale preludes

Clairon (French, 'clarion') A 4 ft chorus reed in French organs; the octave of the *Trompette* (q.v.)

Clarabella A sweet-toned open wood flute of 8 ft pitch; invented by J. C. Bishop of London, *c.* 1840. See also *Stopped Diapason*

Claribel flute A pure-toned flute stop of 8 ft and, less frequently, 4 ft pitch. Much used by Willis in his great organs, who made them of metal from middle C and harmonic above g^1. See *Harmonic* and *Harmonic flute*

Clarinet A solo reed with half-length cylindrical bodies, imitating the orchestral instrument. Usually found in choir or solo organs. In 16 ft pitch, as a bass or double clarinet, it is often duplexed on the pedals, and is an effective double reed in small swell organs

Clarinet flute A small-scale stopped flute, voiced to yield prominent odd-numbered harmonics and consequently a

163

clarinet-like tone. Occasionally found in Victorian organs by Gray and Davison

Clarion mixture A brilliant, high-pitched mixture designed to stand in place of the clarion 4 ft chorus reed. As made by Walker in the late nineteenth century it can be used as a flue chorus mixture with splendid effect

Clear flute An open wood stop of 4 ft pitch

Concert flute An imitation of the orchestral flute. See *Orchestral*

Cone Gamba See *Spitzgamba*

Contra A prefix indicating that a stop is of sub-unison (16 ft manual, 32 ft pedal) pitch; e.g., contra fagotto. See also *Double*, *Sub*

Contrabass (French: contrebass) A pungent-toned 16 ft flue stop, of open wood or metal, voiced to imitate the 'bite' of an orchestral bouble bass, and to give definition to the 16 ft pedal line

Coppel, Copel, Copula See *Koppel*

Cor anglais A solo reed of melancholy tone, voiced to imitate the orchestral instrument. The pipes are of metal, narrow-scaled, and topped by a bell formed of two truncated cones

Cor de nui (French; German: Nachthorn) A wide-scaled flute, open or stopped, of 8 ft, 4 ft or 2 ft pitch

Cormorne (French) See *Krummhorn*

Cornet In strict usage a five-rank compound stop (usually of short compass, from middle C) consisting of wide-scale pipes: stopped 8 ft, open metal 4 ft, $2\frac{2}{3}$ ft, 2 ft and $1\frac{3}{5}$ ft. The combined effect of these five ranks is a bold reed-like sonority, useful for solos either alone or with other stops, and for strengthening the weak trebles of low-pressure chorus reeds. Sometimes the 8 ft rank is omitted. The term 'cornet', like *Sesquialtera* (q.v.), has been used imprecisely at various periods to denote any stop containing a tierce. In British organs of the late seventeenth and eighteenth centuries, to save soundboard space, the great organ cornet was often placed on its own raised soundboard. It was then known as the 'mounted cornet'

Cornett   A pedal solo reed of 4 ft or 2 ft pitch

Corno di bassetto   (Italian, 'basset-horn') A solo reed of clarinet type. Many fine examples were made by Father Willis

Corno dolce.   See *Dolce*

Cornopean   The name commonly given to the swell 8 ft chorus trumpet. The original cornopean was invented by William Hill and intended to imitate the round and mellow tone of the cornet à pistons. See also *Horn*

Cremona   A solo stop of clarinet-type in old English organs. A derivation of Krummhorn or cormorne

Cromorne   (French) see *Krummhorn*

Cymbale   (French; German: Zymbel) A very high-pitched mixture of octave and fifth-sounding ranks breaking and repeating in pitch at every octave of the compass. The German Terzzymbel contains third-sounding ranks

Cymbelstern   (German, 'cymbal-star') An ornamental wooden star forming part of a decorative organ case, with small bells attached to its points which revolve when the stop is drawn. It is found in German organs of the sixteenth, seventeenth and eighteenth centuries

Decima   (Latin, 'tenth') A tenth-sounding stop: $3\frac{1}{5}$ ft See *Tierce*

Diapason   (Greek: διά πασῶν 'through all' [the notes]) Strictly called *open* diapason in distinction to *stopped* diapason (q.v.). The characteristic foundation tone unique to the organ of which its dominant flue choruses are constructed. The construction of a diapason chorus is explained on page 37. There are very many varieties of diapason tone, depending on the voicing practice of the period and the taste of the maker. The broad classifications covered in the historical survey of Chapter VI include:

(i) early English seventeenth- and eighteenth-century;
(ii) Baroque German;
(iii) Baroque or classical French;
(iv) nineteenth-century German (Schulze type);
(v) nineteenth-century French (Cavaillé-Coll type);
(vi) nineteenth-century British and
(vii) large open diapasons developed in Britain during the late Victorian and Edwardian periods. See also *Diapason phonon, Geigen, Montre, Principal*

Diapason phonon (Greek: διὰ πασῶν φῶνων 'through all the voices') A powerful open diapason of smooth foundational and unblending tone developed by Robert Hope Jones. It is made by raising the wind-pressure and leathering the lips of a large-scale, thick metal stop

Dolce, (Italian, 'sweet') **Dolcan, Corno dolce** The distinctions between stops bearing these names are obscure. The tone can be of a gentle flute-string or a soft, horn-like quality produced by metal pipes with a slight outward taper. Cylindrical and inward-tapered pipes are also used

Doppelflöte (German, 'double flute') A pure-toned, large-scale open flute of wood or metal with two mouths

Double A prefix denoting that a stop is of sub-unison pitch, e.g., manuals: double clarinet 16 ft; pedals: double open diapason 32 ft. See also *Contra, Sub*

Doublette (i) The French counterpart of the *Fifteenth* or *superoctave* 2 ft. (q.v.)
(ii) A two-rank compound stop sounding the fifteenth and the twenty-second

Dulcet A *Dulciana* of 4 ft pitch (q.v.)

Dulcian, Dulzian A soft, small-scale reed stop of bassoon-like tone

Select Glossary of Organ Stops

Dulciana A favourite soft accompanimental stop in British organs, first used by Snetzler at St Margaret, Kings Lynn in 1754. It can be either a narrow-scale, diminutive open diapason or more string-like in quality

Dulciana mixture A compound stop composed of dulciana pipes

Dulciana principal A soft *Principal* or a *Dulcet* 4 ft (q.v.)

Duodecima (Latin, 'twelfth') A *Twelfth* or *Octave quint* 2⅔ ft (q.v.)

Echo (i) A prefix to a stop name implying a quieter version of a normal stop, e.g., echo bourdon, echo trumpet.
(ii) A manual division. See page 60

English horn See *Cor anglais*

Erzähler (German. 'narrator') A soft stop of *Gemshorn* type invented by E. M. Skinner of the U.S.A., in 1904 (q.v.)

Fagotto See *Bassoon*

Fernflöte (German, 'distant' or 'echo' flute) A rarely found small-scale quiet flute of tapered construction

Fifteenth, Superoctave The 2 ft member of a diapason chorus on the manuals and the 4 ft member on the pedals. See also *Doublette*

Flachflöte (German, 'flat flute') An open metal flute of 8 ft, 4 ft or 2 ft pitch; either cylindrical or conical. Sometimes of wooden pipes with rectangular ('flat') cross-section

Flageolet An open metal flute, 2 ft or 1 ft. The stops labelled 'flageolet 2 ft' provided by Father Willis in his swell organs were silvery diapason *Fifteenths* (q.v.)

Flautino A 2 ft open flute

Flügelhorn (German, 'winged horn' or kind of bugle) A wide-scale 8 ft reed stop of horn-like timbre

Flûte bouchée harmonique (French, 'stopped harmonic flute') A flute of *Zauberflöte* type (q.v.)

Flûte à cheminée (French; English: chimney flute), See *Rohrflöte*

Flûte conique (French; English: cone flute) See *Spitzflöte*

Flûte harmonique (French) See *Harmonic flute*

Fourniture (French; English: furniture) A *ripieno* mixture strictly of octave and fifth-sounding ranks, though third-sounding ranks have been introduced in British stops of this name at various periods

French horn In eighteenth-century British organs a low-pressure reed stop of stifled trumpet quality. In modern organs a heavy-pressure reed voiced very smoothly to imitate a quieter mood of the orchestral horn

Full mixture A chorus mixture of octave and fifth-sounding ranks, but of lower pitch than the *Sharp mixture* (q.v.)

Gamba A long-standing abbreviation of *Viola da gamba* (q.v.) The name can mean almost any kind of string tone. See also *Spitzgamba*

Gambette A 4 ft gamba

Gedeckt (German 'stopped') A stopped flute of wood or metal and made in all octave pitches from 32 ft to 2 ft. In pre-1850 organs the scale is wide and the tone full. The later *Lieblich Gedeckt* (*Gedact* or *Gedackt*) is of small scale and gentle tone (q.v.) See also *Stillgedeckt, Zauberflöte, Stopped diapason, Bourdon*

Gedecktpommer (German) A Gedeckt overblown so that the twelfth is prominent. See *Quintaten*

Geigen (German, 'violin'), **Geigen principal**, **Geigen diapason**, **Violin diapason** A narrow-scale open diapason voiced with a pronounced string quality. It is frequently found in swell organs and sometimes on the great, where it makes a good double

Gemshorn (German, 'goat's horn') An open metal flue stop of tapered construction and a beautiful and distinctive flute-string timbre. Strictly a member of the half-stopped class. The true Gemshorn is of wide scale, less pointed than the *Spitzflöte* (q.v.) and inclining more to flutiness. In most British organs, however, the Gemshorn is of narrow scale and silvery tone

Gravissima (Latin, 'very heavy') A pedal flue stop in which a resultant 64 ft tone is generated by coupling a *Quint* rank of 21⅓ ft pitch with a rank of 32 ft pitch (q.v.)

Gross (German, 'large') A prefix indicating that a stop is either of large scale or double pitch, e.g., Gross Geigen 16 ft

Harmonia aetheria (Greek, 'heavenly harmony') An echo mixture of small-scale pipes

Harmonic A prefix to a stop name indicating that it is constructed on the harmonic principle. In flue pipes the pipe bodies are double or a multiple of their normal length, and overblown so that the note yielded is the first upper partial proper to the type of pipe. Thus, a harmonic open flue pipe is double length and sounds the octave as its chief tone; a harmonic stopped flue pipe is triple length and yields the twelfth (the first upper partial of a stopped pipe). The production of the harmonic note is encouraged by boring small holes at appropriate distances in the bodies (about half-way in open pipes, and two-thirds or three-fifths in closed ones). In harmonic reeds the tongue, shallot etc, are of normal size, but the resonator is double length. The hole is unnecessary because the energy of the reed blown by high-pressure wind is sufficient to force the air-column to vibrate in segments without other inducement. The tone of harmonic stops is fuller and richer than stops of normal construction, though of inferior blending quality. See *Harmonic flute* and *Zauberflöte*

Harmonic bass See *Acoustic Bass*

Harmonic flute An open metal cylindrical flute, constructed on the harmonic principle (see *Harmonic*, above), invented by

169

Cavaillé-Coll. It was much copied in Britain where, until recently, it was the standard great organ 4 ft flute. The very 'pure' tone does not blend with diapasons. See also *Stopped diapason*

Harmonics A small-scale compound stop, usually consisting of 17th, 19th, flat 21st and 22nd at CC. The intention is that it should reinforce the natural harmonics of the diapasons. The effect is usually rather 'scratchy' and unpleasant

Hautboy (French: hautbois; German and Italian: oboe) A popular 8 ft reed stop in British swell organs, with a tone quality reminiscent of the orchestral instrument but not imitative of it. The resonators are narrow-scale conical, sometimes with a flare towards the top. Hautboys are also made in 4 ft and 16 ft pitch, in the latter form being an excellent double reed in small swell organs

Hohlflöte (German) A round-toned open flute of medium scale; properly of wood

Horn When not deliberately imitative of the orchestral horn (see *French horn*), this reed stop (usually on the swell) is of somewhat stifled trumpet tone. Often synonymous with *Cornopean* (q.v.)

Horn diapason A medium-scale open diapason with a somewhat hard tone quality, due in many cases to the practice of cutting slots at the back of the pipe tops

Keraulophon(e) (from three Greek words meaning horn, flute and voice) An obsolete narrow-scale flue stop, much provided in the nineteenth century by Gray & Davison. The tone is a quiet flute-string quality

Klein (German, 'small') An adjective denoting an octave or small-scale version of a stop, e.g., Kleingedeckt

Koppel, Koppelflöte, Coppel, Copel, Copula (German: Koppeln, 'to couple') A clear-toned flute intended to bind together the tones of other stops. It is usually made of cylindrical metal pipes with inward tapered tops, though it is sometimes a *Gedeckt* (q.v.)

Select Glossary of Organ Stops

Krummhorn (German, 'crooked horn'); French: cormorne or cromorne) A small-scale reed stop with cylindrical tubes giving a penetrating clarinet-like tone. It is equally useful for solo or ensemble use, and is an essential voice for the realization of much of the French and German baroque repertoire. It is also a particularly effective ensemble stop in 16 ft pitch. See also *Cremona*

Larigot (French: l'arigot, 'the flageolet') A manual flute mutation stop of $1\frac{1}{3}$ ft pitch useful for synthetic tone-building Also a pedal mutation of $2\frac{2}{3}$ ft pitch

Lieblich (German, 'lovely') A prefix indicating especial sweetness of tone; usually applied to *Gedeckts* (q.v.)

Lieblich Gedeckt, Gedackt, Gedact (German) A soft small-scale stopped flute of wood or metal and sweet and gentle tone. Introduced into Britain by Edmund Schulze in 1851 and subsequently a favourite in swell and choir organs, where it appears in various pitches: Lieblich Bourdon 16 ft, Lieblich Flöte 4 ft and Lieblich Piccolo 2 ft. See also *Stopped diapason*

Major bass A pedal open diapason 16 ft pitch usually of large-scale wood. The name is sometimes applied to pedal open flue stops of 32 ft pitch

Mixture (German: Mixtur) The nature and function of mixtures has been outlined on pages 37–40. The term is commonly used in two senses. (i) Loosely, as a generic term denoting any kind of chorus compound stop regardless of composition.
(ii) Strictly, denoting a chorus compound stop consisting of octave- and fifth-sounding ranks only. See also *Clarion mixture, Cornet, Cymbale, Full Mixture, Harmonics, Plein jeu, Rauschquint, Ripieno, Sesquialtera, Sharp mixture*

Montre (French, 'show') The French counterpart of the British open diapason and the German Prinzipal. Such stops formed the show pipes of the French organ, from which the stop derived its name. The seventeenth- and eighteenth-century montres are described on page 99. During the nineteenth century Cavaillé-

Coll developed a new type of montre with a pronounced string quality

Mounted Cornet   See *Cornet*

Nachthorn   (German) See *Cor de nuit*

Nasard, Nazard   (French; German: Nasat) A manual flute mutation of 2⅔ ft pitch intended primarily for synthetic tone-building. Also a pedal chorus mutation of 5⅓ ft pitch

Nason   A stopped 4 ft flute with a pronounced twelfth giving it a mildly nasal quality

Nineteenth   A mutation stop of 1⅓ ft pitch manuals and 2⅔ ft pedals. It may be either a separate ingredient of a diapason chorus or a flute (solo) mutation, in which case it is more appropriately named *Larigot* (q.v.)

Oboe   See *Hautboy*

Octave   (i) A prefix to a stop name implying that it is the 4 ft version of an 8 ft manual stop or the 8 ft version of a 16 ft pedal one.
(ii) A name sometimes given to the *octave* member of a diapason chorus—of 8 ft, 4 ft or 2 ft pitch, depending on whether the chorus is based on a 16 ft, 8 ft or 4 ft pitch foundation. As all British great diapason choruses are based on 8 ft pitch, the chief 4 ft diapason member is sometimes called 'octave' as an alternative to 'principal' (q.v.)

Octave quint   The 2⅔ ft member of a diapason chorus. An alternative name to *Twelfth* (q.v.)

Octavin   An open metal flue stop of 2 ft or 1 ft pitch

Open diapason   See *Diapason*

Ophicleide   (derived from Greek words meaning serpent and key) A powerful high-pressure chorus reed of rich but refined tone: usually a pedal 16 ft reed

Orchestral   A prefix indicating that a stop is supposed to imitate as closely as possible an orchestral prototype. The orchestral basson and oboe have narrower tubes than the normal organ type. Attempts have been made to imitate the orchestral flute (concert flute) by employing small-scale cylindrical open wooden tubes with narrow mouths

Piccolo   A 2 ft or 1 ft open flute

Plein jeu   (French: 'full chorus') a chorus mixture of octave- and fifth-sounding ranks; sometimes containing six or seven ranks and breaking to unison and sub-unison pitches in the treble

Posaune   A trumpet-type chorus reed; 8 ft manuals, 16 ft pedals

Prestant   The French equivalent of the British 4 ft *Octave* or *Principal* (q.v.) In Dutch organs it is usually a principal of 16 ft or 8 ft pitch

Principal   (German: Prinzipal) A stop of open diapason tone. Use of the name includes:
 (i) most commonly, the 4 ft member of a diapason chorus, as an alternative to *Octave* (q.v.)
 (ii) the *basic* diapason member of a chorus, the pitch varying according to whether the chorus is based on a 16 ft, 8 ft, 4 ft or 2 ft foundation; and
 (iii) open diapasons of 8 ft pitch manuals and 16 ft pedals

Quartane   See *Rauschquint*

Quarte de nasard   (French) A flute stop sounding a fourth above the nasard $2\frac{2}{3}$ ft (i.e., 2 ft pitch), primarily intended for synthetic tone-building with the solo mutations

Quint   (Latin: quintus, 'fifth'; French and German: Quinte; Italian: quinta) A mutation stop of $10\frac{2}{3}$ pitch pedals and $5\frac{1}{3}$ ft pitch manuals, being part of the 32 ft and 16 ft harmonic series respectively. A manual quint $5\frac{1}{3}$ ft combines with 8 ft stops to produce resultants that strengthen the 16 ft tone. A pedal quint $10\frac{2}{3}$ similarly produces 32 ft resultants

Quintadena   A small or octave *Quintaten* (q.v.)

173

N*

Quintaten, Quintaton, Quintade   A stopped flute voiced so that the twelfth speaks almost as prominently as the foundation tone. In 16 ft pitch it is an excellent manual flue double

Rauschquint   (German, 'rustling quint') A two-rank diapason mixture sounding the twelfth and fifteenth. The interval of a fourth accounts for the alternative name 'quartane'. Also called 'grave mixture'

Recorder   (German: Blockflöte) An open metal flute of widish scale intended to imitate the instrument of the same name. Sometimes made with a slight inward taper

Regal   A reed stop with very short resonators unrelated in length to the pitch of the reed. The tone is generally colourful and bucolic. See also *Apfelregal, Barpfeife*

Resultant   See *Acoustic Bass*

Ripieno   (Italian, 'filling up') A mixture for adding body to a chorus rather than brilliance

Rohrflöte   (German: French: flûte à chiminée; English: chimney flute; sometimes half-anglicized as rohr flute) A half-stopped metal flute with a chimney fixed into the stopper. The chimney introduces a lamination of even numbered harmonics into the odd-numbered make-up of the stopped pipe beside adding a subtle formant of its own. The tone is characteristically colourful and liquid. Rohrburden, Rohrgedeckt and Rohrpommer are similarly treated

Rohr Schalmai   (German, 'chimney shawm') A variation of the Schalmai (chalumeau), in which the main part of the cylindrical pipe body is connected to the block by a thin, chimney-like stalk. The tone is pungent, hollow and intense

Salicet   A 4 ft salicional

Salicional   (Latin: salix, 'willow') A narrow-scale open metal cylindrical stop with a delicate, stringy-tone quality Sometimes a diminutive diapason

Schalmai See *Chalumeau, Rohr Schalmai*

Scharf (German, 'sharp'; Dutch: scherp) A brilliant high-pitched mixture of octave and fifth-sounding ranks

Septième A flat seventh-sounding mutation stop: $2\frac{2}{7}$ ft and $1\frac{1}{7}$ ft manuals; $4\frac{4}{7}$ ft pedals. In British organs its usual form is a soft flute mutation $1\frac{1}{7}$ ft in enclosed choir organs for synthetic tone-building

Sesquialtera, Sexquialtera (Latin: sesqui, a ratio of 3 to 2) Strictly, a two-rank compound stop sounding the twelfth and seventeenth, usable as chorus thickening matter or for solo colouring. In classical German and Dutch organs the ranks are of diapason scale, adding a reedy richness to the clean-toned octave and fifth chorus. Some sesquialteras have higher-pitched ranks in the bass, breaking to 12 and 17 at middle C, at which point the effective solo range begins. In old English organs the sesquialtera was a chorus mixture of three or four ranks including the seventeenth, and subsequently the name has been loosely used. See also *Cornet*

Seventeenth See *Tierce*

Sext A compound stop sounding the twelfth and seventeenth after the manner of the *Sesquialtera* (q.v.)

Sharp mixture A chorus mixture of higher pitch than the *Full mixture* (q.v.) with which it is usually found

Sifflöte (German, perhaps 'whistling flute' (cf. French siffler, 'to whistle')) An open metal flute, 2 ft or 1 ft; but sometimes a flute mutation $1\frac{1}{3}$ ft

Spillflöte, Spindelflöte (German, 'spindle flute') An open metal flute (8 ft, 4 ft or 2 ft) with fairly narrow-scale cylindrical bodies with inward tapered tops (e.g., a smaller-scale type of *Koppel* (q.v.), of which it may fairly be described as a brighter version). Strictly, a member of the half-stopped class

Spitzflöte (German, 'pointed flute'; French: flûte à fuseau; English: spire flute or cone flute; sometimes half-anglicized as spitz flute) An open metal flue stop of tapered construction, but more pointed than the true *Gemshorn* (q.v.), and with more harmonic development. A well-blending hybrid flute-string tone. Commonly of 8 ft, 4 ft or 2 ft pitch; but 16 ft and 32 ft specimens are known. Strictly a member of the half-stopped class (see also *Spillflöte*)

Spitzgamba (German, 'pointed gamba') **Cone gamba** A gamba with tapered pipes

Stentorphone (from the Greek: Stentor, the loud-voiced herald before Troy) A large-scale, loud, open flue stop of no artistic value, found in large American organs

Stillgedeckt A quiet *Gedeckt* (q.v.)

Stopped bass The lowest twelve notes of a stopped diapason drawing separately to provide a common bass to one or more other stops terminating at tenor C. Still to be found in some old organs built before about 1900

Stopped diapason A stopped flute; the British counterpart of the German *Gedeckt* and the French *Bourdon* (q.v.) It was the standard flute tone in British organs before the introduction during the nineteenth century of the *Clarabella,* the *Harmonic flute* and the *Lieblich Gedeckt* (q.v.) The old British stopped diapasons were usually made of wood, though they were occasionally of metal chimney flute construction. On the great organ were combined with the open diapason to form the foundation tone of the flue chorus

Suabe flute An open wood flute of 4 ft pitch and sweet tone, invented by William Hill. It has inverted mouths (i.e., bevelled on the inside instead of the outside)

Sub A prefix synonymous with *Contra* or *Double* (q.v.)

Sub-bass (German: Subbass; French: soubasse) A *Bourdon* of 16 ft or 32 ft pitch (q.v.)

Superoctave The 2 ft member of a diapason chorus; also called *Fifteenth* (q.v.). See also *Doublette*

Sylvestrina   A soft flute-string tone stop of German origin and tapered construction

Tenoroon   A name used in nineteenth-century British organs to denote a 16 ft *Bourdon* or *Open diapason* (q.v.) terminating at tenor C. Since the name derives from an instrument known as the tenor bassoon it may have been applied initially to reed stops

Tertian, Terzian   A compound stop containing the interval of a minor third; normally two ranks: seventeenth and nineteenth at CC

Tibia   (Latin, 'pipe') A pure-toned open flute. The term is generally associated with an unblending tone quality of no serious musical value, developed by Hope Jones and prominent in the palette of the cinema organ—a large-scale, heavy-winded stop with an enlarged foundation tone and minimum harmonic development

Tibia clausia   A name given by Hope Jones to a *Bourdon* (q.v.)

Tierce   (French, 'a third'; German: terz; Italian: decima settima) Sometimes called 'seventeenth' in British organs. A mutation stop of $1\frac{3}{5}$ ft manuals; $3\frac{1}{5}$ ft and rarely $6\frac{2}{5}$ ft pedals; being the fifth harmonic and the seventeenth interval in the 8 ft, 16 ft and 32 ft series respectively. It can be either of diapason tone for chorus colouring, or of flute or Gemshorn tone for synthetic tone-building, in which form it is usually found in choir or positive divisions

Tremulant, Tremolo   A device for inducing a waving or vibrato effect in the sound of organ pipes. There are two systems: (i) a rotary fan which disturbs the air over the pipes, and (ii) a pulsating pneumatic motor which disturbs the wind supply

Tromba   (Italian, 'trumpet') A heavy-winded chorus reed of powerful smooth tone—the tonal opposite of a brilliant free-toned trumpet. Originally the Italian name for stops of the trumpet class

Select Glossary of Organ Stops

Trombone A chorus pedal reed of 16 ft or 32 ft pitch (contra trombone) or a manual chorus reed of 16 ft or 8 ft pitch. The name generally implies some kind of trumpet quality; though it is sometimes given to a 16 ft manual *Tromba* (q.v.)

Trompette (French, 'trumpet') The French name for an 8 ft chorus *Trumpet* (q.v.) Used in British organs it implies a stop of French character, that is, with more harmonic development and less body than a normal British trumpet See also *Clairon*

Trompette en chamade (French) A reed stop with tubes projecting horizontally, sometimes from the front of the organ case, as in Spanish organs

Trumpet The standard chorus reed in British organs. The use of a family of trumpets in the full swell is explained on page 40. See also *Cornopean*

Tuba (Latin, 'trumpet'), **Tuba mirabilis**, Latin ('wonderful trumpet'), **Tuba magna** ('great trumpet') A loud, high-pressure reed stop with a full-bodied, trumpet-like tone, intended primarily for solo use

Tuba clarion A 4 ft tuba

Twelfth The $2\frac{2}{3}$ ft member of a manual diapason chorus, and the $5\frac{1}{3}$ ft member of a pedal one; being the third harmonic of the 8 ft and 16 ft series respectively

Twenty-second A diapason flue stop; 1 ft manuals, 2 ft pedals

Unda maris (Latin, 'wave of the sea') A restful undulating stop of the *Voix céleste* type (q.v.) Properly, it consists of a rank of quiet flute tone tuned slightly sharp or flat to the pitch of the organ so as to beat restfully with another rank of similar quality; but pipes of *Dulciana* or *Gamba* tone are sometimes used (q.v.)

Untersatz (German) A sub-bourdon. See *Sub-bass*

Viol (French and German: viole) A generic name for small-scale keen-toned string stops. Often qualified by other terms

Viola da gamba (Italian: gamba, 'leg') In old organs a stop intended to imitate the viola da gamba, a fiddle. Nowadays it can mean almost any stop of string tone, though generally less attenuated than the *Viol* type (q.v.)

Viola d'amour A refined-toned string stop of 8 ft or 4 ft pitch

Viole céleste (French, 'heavenly viol') An undulating stop of viole pipes. See *Voix céleste*

Viole d'orchestre (French, 'orchestral viol') A soft, open metal string stop of very narrow-scale and extremely attenuated tone. Invented by William Thynne, of Mitchell and Thynne, London, in 1885. An exaggerated tone of poor blending quality

Viole sourdine (French, 'muted viol') An ultra-delicate and subdued string stop of the *Viole d'orchestre* type (q.v.). Also invented by Thynne, 1885

Violin An open metal 8 ft string stop, supposed to imitate the tone of the violin

Violin diapason See *Geigen*

Violoncello, Cello (Italian; French: violoncelle) An 8 ft string stop, open wood or metal, imitating to some extent the tone of the stringed instrument. A frequent 8 ft pedal stop in Victorian organs

Violone (Italian; French and German: violon) An open flue stop of mild string tone, sometimes usable as a quiet alternative bass to the *Bourdon* (q.v.) Also a manual double, synonymous with contra gamba or contra viola

Voix céleste (French, 'heavenly voice') A string stop tuned slightly sharp or flat to the pitch of the organ so that, when drawn with an appropriate 'in tune' stop (e.g., viola da gamba, salicional, echo gamba), it produces a pleasant waving of tone. Such stops are known as 'undulating stops'. The céleste rank does not normally extend below tenor C. See also *Unda maris, Vox angelica, Viole céleste*

Vox angelica (Latin, 'angelic voice') An undulating stop of *dulciana* or *Salicional* tone (q.v.) See *Voix céleste*

Vox humana (Latin, 'human voice'; French: voix humaine; Italian: voce umana) An 8 ft reed stop with one-eighth length cylindrical resonators producing a thin, 'throaty' tone. A refined relic of the old regal (Schnarrwerk) class. The vox humana is useful for colouring other stops or, if not too soft, as a solo stop in seventeenth and eighteenth-century French and German music. In Italian organs the voce umana can be a diapason undulating stop. See also *Baryton*

Waldflöte (German, 'wood' or 'forest' flute; Dutch: woudfliut) An open flute, usually of wood; 8 ft, 4 ft and occasionally of 2 ft pitch

Waldhorn (German, 'forest horn'; original German name for the French horn) A reed stop of full-bodied horn-like timbre. Used as a swell organ double reed in some Willis organs of the present century

Zauberflöte (German, 'magic flute') Invented by William Thynne, 1885. A *Gedeckt* (q.v.) treated on the harmonic principle (see *Harmonic*)

Zink, Zinck, Zinken A reed stop, usually of 2 ft pitch on the pedals, with a bright and penetrating tone. The name is derived from an old trumpet-like instrument

Zymbel See *Cymbale*

Select Bibliography

The following short selection from the large bibliography of the organ is recommended as a beginning for the reader who, it is hoped, will have been stimulated to delve more deeply into the subject. Only works in English are mentioned. For deeper investigation, the extensive bibliography in the third edition of W. L. Sumner's *The Organ, Its Evolution, Principles of Construction and Use* (1962) is highly recommended. Among British periodicals, *The Organ,* published quarterly since 1921, is an invaluable and fascinating source of historical and other information about all aspects of the instrument.

Blanton, J. E., *The Organ in Church Design* (Albany, Texas, 1958)

Bonavia Hunt, N. A., *Modern Organ Stops* (London, 1923)

Clutton, C. and Niland, A., *The British Organ* (London, 1963, 3rd impression, 1966)

Goode, J. C., *Pipe Organ Registration* (New York, 1964)

Hopkins, E. J., and Rimbault, E. F., *The Organ, Its History and Construction* (London, 1855, 3rd edition, 1877)

Irwin, S., *Dictionary of Pipe Organ Stops* (New York, 1962)

Jeans, J., *Science and Music* (London, 1937)

Norman, H., and Norman, H. J., *The Organ Today* (London, 1966)

Sumner, W. L., *The Organ, Its Evolution, Principles of Construction and Use* (London, 1952, 3rd edition, 1962)

Sumner, W. L., 'Arp Schnitger' *Organ Institute Quarterly* (Andover, Mass., 1955–1956)

Select Bibliography

Sumner, W. L., 'The Organ of Bach' *Hinrichsen's Eighth Music Book* (London, 1956)

Sumner, W. L., 'Silbermann and His Work' *Hinrichsen's Eighth Music Book* (London, 1956)

Sumner, W. L., *Father Henry Willis* (London, 1957)

Sumner, W. L., *Bach's Organ-Registration* (London, 1961)

Williams, P. L., *The European Organ* (London, 1966)

Periodicals
  Britain:
    Journal of the Incorporated Society of Organ Builders
    Musical Opinion
    Musical Times
    The Organ
  U.S.A.:
    The American Organist
    The Diapason
    The Organ Institute Quarterly
    The Tracker

Index

Stop names are not included. For these see the alphabetical glossary beginning on page 161.
References to figure illustrations are in bold type.
The upper case Roman numerals refer to the plate illustrations.

Index

British school of organ building,
111–33
classical revival, 131–2
comparison with foreign schools,
112
innovations of Willis and Schulze,
125 ff
19th-century, 122–4
principal composers, 115
registration, late 17th and 18th
century, 120–22
restoration of historic organs,
132–3
Restoration period to 1800, 115–
122
20th-century, 129–31
Brustwerk, 85 ff
Buckfast Abbey, 75
Bull, 43
Buxtehude, 43
Byfield, John, 117

Calvière, 100
Cappel, Schnitger organ, vi, 87, 90
Cavaillé-Coll, Aristide, 10, 97, 106,
107 ff, 125 ff, 166, 170, 171–2
influence on Willis, 106
stop control system, 109
Chair organ, 114
Choir and positive organs, 51–4
Choir organ, 44, 51–4, 114
Chorus structure, 32–6
Classical organ,
general definition, 24
in 18th-century Germany, 96
Classical revival, 110
Clavier des bombardes, 59
Clérambault, Louis Nicholas, 100
Cliquot (organ builder), 101
Combination pistons, *see* thumb
pistons
Combined actions, 18
Compass,
British, late 17th, 18th centuries,
116
Italian, 17th century, 104
manual, 70
pedal, 71

Compound stops, *see* Mixtures
Compton Organ Company, 69, 131
Console, 12, 68
Coventry Cathedral, II
London, St Mary Rotherhithe,
VII
London, St Vedast, Foster Lane,
III
modern Willis, 69
stop-key, V
stop-tablet, VI
Wimborne Minster, IV
Control of the British organ, 68–75
Corbeil, Ile de France, St-Spire, 97
Couperin, François, 100
Couplers, 7, 61–2
combination, 72
Coventry Cathedral, 69
console, II
Crescendo pedal, 73–5
Cristofori, 103
Croft, W., 115
Cromorne en taille, 101

Dallam family, 115
Dallam, Thomas, 112–13
Danby, Nicholas, xxii
de Grigny, Nicholas, 100
Descant manual, 82
Diapason (or Principal) chorus,
British late 17th–18th centuries,
116
British pre-Commonwealth, 113
Cavaillé-Coll, 108
French classical, 99
German 15th century, 85
Gothic, 81
Harrison, 130
Hill 1840, 124
Italian 17th century, 105
modern British choir-positive, 53
„   „   great, 45–7
„   „   pedal, 56
„   „   swell, 49
Schulze, 128
Willis, 126
Diapason tone, 29
Direct-electric action, 8, 16

184

Index

Diruta, Girolamo, *Il Transilvano*, 105
Division principle, 83
Divisions, 6
Dixon, Lt. Col. George, 130
Donnington, Robert, *The Interpretation of Early Music*, 95
Double organ, 114, 154
Double pitch, 33
Double touch cancelling, 73
Double touch pistons, 73
Downes, Ralph, 131
Drawstops, 6, 69
Dynamics, in Bach's organ music, 94

Echo organ, 60–1
  Liverpool Anglican Cathedral, 60
  Norwich Cathedral, 60
  Old English, 116
  Tewkesbury Abbey, 61
  Westminster Abbey, 61
Electro-pneumatic action, 13–18
  primary action, 6
  Roosevelt system, 7
  with slider chest, 5
Ely Cathedral organ, 130
Emery, Walter, *On the registration of Bach's Preludes and Fugues*, 152
Enclosed divisions, 8
Extension organ, registration on, 147
Extension system, 16, 63–7

Floating divisions, 45
Flue pipes, 1, 9, 10, 20
  method of tone production, 21–5
Flute chorus, 41
Flute tone, 29
Flutes, on great organ, 45
Forkel, J. N., *On Johann Seb. Bach's Life, Genius and Works*, 94
Formant, 28
Foundation tone, 29
Fouquet, 100
Franck, César, 43, 106, 107, 109, 155, 156

Chorale No. 1 in E major, 156
Chorale No. 3 in A minor, 156
Prière, 156
Freiburg University, 110
French organ building school,
  19th-century symphonic, 107–9
  17th and 18th centuries, 97–102
Frescobaldi, 103
  Canzoni, 154
  Toccata per l'Elevazione, 105, 153

Gauntlett, Dr H. J., 123
General cancel piston, 73
General pistons, 72
German Baroque school, 84–96
  compared with modern British organ, 88
  composers, 86
  dynamics, 94
  evolution, 85
  flute group, 90
  principal chorus, 89–90
  reeds, 91–2
  registration, 92
German 19th-century school, 109, 110
Ghent, 82
Gibbons, Orlando, 154
Gigault, Nicholas, 100
Gillingham, Michael, xxii
Gothic organ, 80–3
  in Italy, 84
Grand jeu, 47, 100, 153–4
Grand jeu de tierce, 101
Grand organ, 45, 81, 82
Grant, Degens and Bradbeer (organ builders), 132
Gray and Davison (organ builders), VII, 125, 150, 151, 170
Great organ, 6, 44, 45–8
Green, M. (composer), 115, 119
Green, Samuel (organ builder), vi
Guilmant, 108, 109
Gurlitt, Willibald, 110

Haarlem, St Bavo, vi, 86, 96
Halberstad Cathedral, 82
Hamburg, St Jacob, 85

Index

Index

Index